The Memoirs of
Alexander Brodie

Today the remnants of stone walls are all that mark the location of the house and farmstead where pioneer settler Alexander Brodie came of age in pre-Confederation Canada, north of Toronto. (Photos: John Steckley)

The Memoirs of
Alexander Brodie

EDITED AND ANNOTATED BY
John Steckley

Rock's Mills Press
Oakville, Ontario
2019

Published by
Rock's Mills Press
www.rocksmillspress.com

Copyright © 2019 by John Steckley.
All rights reserved. Published by arrangement with the editor.

For information, please contact Rock's Mills Press at customer.service@rocksmillspress.com.

ISBN-13: 978-1-77244-173-4

Alexander Anderson Brodie (1826–1916)

Alexander Anderson Brodie (1826–1916) is my great-great-great-uncle. His younger brother Charles was my great-great-grandfather. Charles' daughter, Harriet Jane Brodie, married my great-grandfather Abram Steckley. I have known of Uncle Alex's existence since I was a child, and first read parts of this memoir when I was a young adult. The land upon which the Brodies settled was best known to me as a place for picnics with my grandparents, Jack and Eva Steckley, although they did not live on the land, but in the nearby town of Stouffville, northeast of Toronto.

Uncle Alex was well-educated, although he never attended university. His mother, a teacher back home in Peterhead in the northeast of Scotland, taught children, and she clearly intended for her children to be well-read, which Uncle Alex certainly was. The memoir, written in 1906, is spiced with the classical allusions as well as references to writers of the time, with quotations in Latin (sometimes misspelled), mentions of Greek gods, and even a reference to one Welsh prince.

Like the writings of other well-educated settlers who told the story of early Ontario, his work is sprinkled throughout with the poetry of his time, the work of 14 writers of the 18th and 19th centuries, the vast majority of them Scottish, and a few English. Six of them had died before Uncle Alex was born. All but one, the mysterious Agnes E. Mitchell who wrote "When the Cows Come Home," were male. Visibly missing from the collection is any work by Robbie Burns, the national poet of Scotland. I believe that is mainly because Burns had a reputation as a womanizer and a drinker. In the strict Presbyterian environment that Uncle Alex was raised in, that just wouldn't do.

He wasn't a scholar or an academic by any means, but like many an "amateur" of the 19th century he was a keen observer of life. He was clearly reflective concerning his lifelong experiences during a time of tremendous social change, and, as you will see, he had a great memory.

He was a natural story-teller but not a writer, a reflection of his lack of university education. His spelling is not good, and his punctuation is spotty. He makes reference to his changeable spelling in a letter to his niece, Jessie. I found it interesting that one of his spelling mistakes is one I used to commit, spelling "immediately" as "immeadiately," which I still sometimes did as an undergraduate. Trying to edit with a light hand, I have inserted the correct spelling in the body of the text, but have footnoted Uncle Alex's spelling with the indication "[AB]." And I have often silently inserted commas and periods where they belong, but were not included. He was a speaker of stories, a bard. The mistakes made were those of someone more used to the spoken than the written word as a mode of telling stories.

I don't have any idea what this reflects, but he had a habit of dropping the pronominal subject, particularly "I," at the beginning of sentences. At first I noticed it a lot, but once I got accustomed to it, it felt normal to me. (It so far has not affected my own writing, but it came close.) I did not change this, as it seemed to me that doing so would have taken away something of the flavour of the original text.

I have, however, introduced headings to give the reader more direction. And some of the chapters were created by my separating different subjects into chapters of their own. I have also added the names of the poems and the poets when he recites their poetry.

Finding the Brodie Gravestone

Uncle Alex left York County in 1865 to live and farm in the vicinity of the village of Dorchester in southwestern Ontario, a few miles east of the city of London. That is where he is buried.

It was a cold, rainy, then snowy, then rainy again day late in March 2016 when my wife Angelika and I went to find Uncle Alex's grave. The wind was blowing up a storm. After much searching and swearing that I know Uncle Alex but not his mother would have appreciated, we found the gravestone. Alex and his wife Mary and their six children (and one mystery Brodie—see the next paragraph) were there. Long-lived, the parents both lived to 90 or more as did three of the children (see below). Four of them were alive when I was born. A cedar, symbol of long life in some cultures, stood proudly above their graves.

But true to the Brodie heritage, the stone also carried a mystery. There was another name on the stone, Lloyde A. Brodie, most probably a grandson, concerning whom we have only a birth date, 1909. Did he disappear in World War II? Was he promised a space by his grandparents to leave his earthly remains in? Perhaps he died on the day he was born.

We decided to put flowers on the grave. It had likely been about a hundred years since he had died. We weren't sure what he would have liked, so we laid two red carnations on the stone.

JOHN STECKLEY
Bolton, Ontario
2019

Inscription on the Brodie Gravestone

Alexander A. Brodie   1826–1916
Mary McRae Brodie   1828–1924

Mary J. Brodie   1859–1955
Charlotte Brodie   1860–1921
Alexandrina Brodie   1863–1957
William Anderson Brodie   1867–1945
George B Brodie   1871–1957
James T. Brodie   1873–1971

Lloyde A. Brodie   1909

Letter to a Niece

Dorchester, Ontario
November 6, 1903
Miss Jessie Brodie

Dear Jessie:

Hear a year ago, that you remarked to someone of the Brodie ilk, that old grandfather Brodie, your great grandfather, was married three times, and had a large family with each wife, I beg to correct you. He was married three times but there was a family only with the first marriage, Barbara Anderson. The second wife was Margret Wilguise or as I have heard my mother pronounced the name "Meggie Wilgies." She was an excellent woman, beloved by all the family. She was dead before my time. The third wife was Annie Groat. I saw her once, while at my grandfather's with my mother. During the day, I went with grandfather to the moor for a load of peat. My impression of Annie was not favourable, she was also much disliked by the family. I think from casual remarks I have heard, Annie feathered her nest pretty well, as she got all the old man had. There was some investigation on the matter at the time of the old man's death, at which Annie was represented by her Advocate and the Minister of the Parish, which ended in a manner unsatisfactory to the rightful heirs.

As I have stated in the Preface to the narrative I sent you, my reason for writing the story is that I am now the oldest member of the family who can remember anything about Peterhead, or the voyage to Quebec and up the St. Lawrence by Durham boat, thence to Toronto. I also thought it would be interesting to some of the kindred who have a desire to know that they have not come from beggars or malefactors.

I have written wholly from memory, what I have seen and heard my father and mother tell about their people. I began with the intention of making a short story but as I proceeded, one incident after another came to mind and I felt an almost irresistible something impel me to tell them. After I had got along so far, Miss Florence Webster suggested getting it printed in a little book. Well, after enquiry I found the cheapest to be fifty cents a page or $35 to $40 for a dozen copies. This was more than I was willing to pay and as none of the nephews or niece, or, my own family, offered a subscription, I gave up the idea of printing. I, however, wrote a copy for Miss Webster and I have done the same for you. You will find many errors in spelling and grammar. My thoughts precede the point of my pen, and I often leave a letter out or put and extra one in where it should not be. As for grammar I write wholly by ear and I find I cannot write two copies alike.

Yours faithfully,
[signed] A. A. Brodie

Foreword by J. A. Brodie

Craigieburn Farm, Lot 2, Concession V, Whitchurch Township was purchased by the Brodie family in 1835. On it then was a log house and a few acres of cleared land. The family and the farm prospered and by 1850 a new native stone house was occupied and by 1880 a modern bank barns with stables etc. was constructed. In 1890, Craigieburn Farm reached its zenith being awarded the "Gold Medal" for York County in that year. Craigieburn declined slowly with farming enterprise of a similar nature in Ontario. The great stone house burned in 1936. The solidly built bank barn and stables are falling in ruins.

In 1936 I received from Jessie Brodie a narrative written by Alexander A. Brodie, her uncle, in 1903. It is the story of the trip of his family in 1835 from Peterhead, Scotland, to a pioneer farm in Ontario, 14 miles north of Toronto. Along with the narrative are miscellaneous notes and references which put together make the story of Craigieburn Farm.

Jessie Brodie was the eldest of four daughters of Dr. William Brodie (Willie) who practiced dentistry for over 40 years on Parliament Street in Toronto, but became best known as a pioneer naturalist of the Toronto area. In 1903, he was appointed Provincial Biologist and Director of the Biological Department of the provincial museum. Jessie was a naturalist in her own right assisting her father in much of the routine work of identification, mounting and preservation of an extensive collection of insects, reptiles, birds and mammals. On the death of her father in 1909, Jessie taught school at Eldersley, Saskatchewan where she died in the late thirties.

For this narrative, we are indebted to Alex A. Brodie, my great uncle, who I met only once at my grandfather's (Charles John) funeral when I was ten years old,—he died shortly after. After leaving "Craigieburn" in 1850 he farmed near Dorchester in Middlesex County. He had two sons and three daughters.[1] The writings which form this story are in the excellent penmanship typical of an earlier era. The documents have, of course, deteriorated over the past 70 years but are still quite legible. Some words are missing at the edge of pages and a few pages are lost. One of two sections relating to family connections in Scotland has been omitted mainly because the sequence of events could not be followed. With these reservations I have reproduced here the precise wording and vernacular of the writer to the best of my ability.

My purpose in making these copies available is to discharge an implied obligation on my part to both Alex A. and Jessie Brodie—with my own we cover three generations of Brodies in Canada. My main purpose is to assure that the story is not lost to this and subsequent generations, so preserve this copy during your lifetime and pass it on to one of the Brodie ilk.

1. This contradicts what is written on the gravestone.

Contents

Alexander Anderson Brodie (1826–1916) by John Steckley ... v
Inscription on the Brodie Gravestone ... vii
Letter to a Niece ... ix
Foreword by J.A. Brodie ... xi
Contents ... xiii

1. Of Early Family, Herding and Prophecies ... 1
2. Life in Peterhead ... 15
3. Planning and Preparing to Leave ... 20
4. Crossing the Atlantic on the *Alert* ... 27
5. Crossing the Atlantic and Arriving in Grosse Isle ... 41
6. Two Boats to the Interior ... 48
7. The Trip Continues to Toronto ... 53
8. Life in Toronto in 1835 and the End of a Friendship ... 59
9. Finding a Home and Settling In ... 71
10. The People of the Area ... 82
11. Making Maple Syrup and Rebellion in Upper Canada ... 92
12. The Indian Raid ... 98
13. The Indian Raid and the Story of the Schells (Shells) in the Mohawk Valley ... 105
14. Mackenzie's Men ... 113
15. Philip Gower ... 123
16. Mr. Button, the Clubines, Philip Gower and the Grenadiers' Grave ... 130
17. Return to Family ... 141
18. A Trip to the St. Lawrence ... 148
19. The Success and Romancing of Dr. John Walters ... 152

References Cited ... 159

Chapter 1
Of Early Family, Herding and Prophecies

[1]Having often been requested by my own family, also Nephews and Nieces, to write up as far as my memory serves me, how and when my parents came to Canada, and any episodes incidental to pioneer life, and what I had heard my father and mother telling of their Forbears.

To give a sketch of family ancestry,[1] for several generations back from little history of family descent, but simply a gleam of light here and there, with long years between, not even amounting to a tradition, is no easy task. When heraldry and titles[2] are unknown, and only the simple annals of the poor (the parish register) to tell of those who once were. No wonder that the common people are so ignorant on family ancestry. Few can connect beyond their grandfather or great grandfather.

In endeavouring to write as my memory serves me, it must be borne in mind I am fourscore years, and al[l]lowing that my memory is fairly reliable for seventy five years back, there doubtless must be many incidents, and tales I have heard I cannot call to mind, that might give some light on the past.

A parchment of family record of my mother's people (carefully preserved by her until her death) went back to early in the seventeenth century. I have a dim remembrance of some of the names but the relation they bore to each other I have not the least recollection. After mother's death this parchment was lost sight of.

Paternal Family

My grandfather, on my father's side, was Alexander Brodie a native of the parish of St. Fergus, in the district of Buchan Aberdeenshire [2] Scotland. All his family being born in the same parish, the farm on which his people had been tenants for many generations back, was called Edney,[3] a short distance from the Village of St. Fergus, think the farm has been annexed to a[d]joining farms since my grandfather's death. Have heard my father say he had heard his father tell that he could remember when a young man, as many as sixty male communicants of the name Brodie in the parish. He had a vague opinion that sometime in the long, long ago his forefathers came from the south of Scotland. Although he claims clanship with the Brodies of Brodie House Morayshire.[4]

1. Alexander Brodie (hereafter AB) "ancestry," here and elsewhere.

2. AB "tittles," here and elsewhere.

3. Udney or Udny.

4. This was the home of Brodie Castle and the various Lords of Brodie over the centuries, including several famous ones that went by the name of Alexander Brodie.

My grandmother on my father's side, whose maiden name was Barbara Anderson, also a native of the same parish. It was very common in Scotland centuries ago, and still continues on many farms to the present day, that families were known and distinguished by the name of their farm. Thus my grandmother's people were known as the Burnshaungy Andersons, they being tenants on that farm for many generations. To these grandparents of mine were born ten children, Annie, Jean, Elizabeth, Mary, Margaret, and Isabella, then Alexander George (who was my father), William and James. I have seen my grandfather. Remember of being at his house once, and going to the moss with him, and a man, for a cart load of peats. Could not say how old I was, but recollected I had no pants. A rather stylish red and white chequered kilt. Grandfather and the man walked. I rode in the cart going to the moss, and held on to the side shelving of the cart or box of the cart. Coming home with the peats a secure place was improvised for me so that I could not fall off, as the load was built up quite high, I had seen Uncle Sandy as we called him, had been at his place. Had seen all my aunts and their husbands. Never saw Uncle [3] Willie nor Jamie [who] were away at sea before I was born.

History of Herding

My father like all Scotch youths (in rural districts), served in his day the common occupation of country boys of herding cows, in the herding season. Attending the parish school in winter customary over a hundred years ago. Herding was an institution in Scotland (and perhaps wherever domestic animals have been kept) of great antiquity. No doubt almost co-eval with our race. But although we can fix no date to the first mention of herding in Scotland, we know by the many allusions to herding in the old songs, and ballads of Scotland, that it has been common since the Doric[5] became the lingual of the lowlands. The herding was not confined to laddies for we know there were[6] herd lassies also.

Logan's Water or Logan's Braes – John Mayne (1759–1836, an excerpt)
By Logan's stream that riuns[7] sae[8] deep
Fer aft wi' glee I've herded sheep
Herded sheep, an gathered slaes[9]
Wi' my dear lad on Logan braes[10]

---

5. Doric is a Scots term for the dialect of English spoken in northeastern Scotland.
6. AB "was", here and in many places were "were" should have been written.
7. Scots Dialect for "runs."
8. Scots Dialect for "so."
9. Scots Dialect for 'sloes' or blackthorn berries.
10. Braes are steep banks or hillsides in Scots dialect.

Up among yon cliffy rocks – William Dudgeon (c. 1753–1813, an excerpt)
Again Up amaing yon cliffy rocks
Sweetly rings the rising echo
To the maid that tends the goats
Lilting oer her native notes
Hark, she sings young Sandy's kind
An he's promised affe to lo'e me
Here's a brooch I ne'er shall tine
Till he's fairly married to me[11]

Although we know little of the inception of herding in Scotland, we know well when it ended. When Lord Broug[ha]m's Act known as the Scotch Elementary Act of 1872 came into full force that all children between the ages of eight and fourteen must attend school. This gave the <u>coup de grace</u> to herding in Scotland, [4] for this was the herding age. There was no doubting a certain romance attached to the herding days, but it was at best a lonely occupation.

Counting Out Rhymes

The Buchan herds,[12] and I suppose all over Scotland had a kind of lore peculiar to the occupation. The blowing of a horn goes back to the days of Garth the Saxon swineherd,[13] but in my father's herding days was almost obsolete. I have heard in passing a herd, herding by the roadside, this dogg[e]rel, Herdy, herdy blow the horn. A'thet kye's[14] amang the corn. The herd laddie was generally equip[p]ed with a stout stick, at least two feet long, an old [handle][15] of a flail made a superexcellent insignia of defence and connection. The name of the owner was generally cut on the end gripped in the hand. There were[16] a number of cuts, or notches, according to following formula:

Twa afore ane, three afore five
First twa an' than twa, an' four come belive;
Now ane than ane, an three at a cast
Double ane an' twice twa, an' Jockie at the last
An Jenny an' her five kye followin' on fast

11. In the end he doesn't marry her.
12. In the Scots dialect of the time "herd" could refer to a person who herded sheep, cattle or goats.
13. Garth the Saxon is a character in Sir Walter Scott's *Ivanhoe*.
14. The word "kye" here refers to a cow. The plural is "kine."
15. Uncle Alex here wrote "suple," for which I can find no meaning.
16. AB "was."

Alexander Paterson in his *Memories of Monquhitter*,[17] where he spent his juvenile years herding, and consequently became an adept in herding lore says, "In conformity with the above not particularly lucid rule, the notches were arranged as below, a rude figure of Jockie occup[y]ing the place of the large dot[18] and ditto of Jenny the small one:

II I [III] IIIII
II II IIII
I I III
X II II (•) IIIII (•)

The notches were designated "Jockies ossen"[19] but I do not know that I ever gave the origin of the rhyme a thought until some twenty years later, when I came across an[20] English version which bore the title of "the Hog's prayer". It was said to be popular in the county of Kent with the swineherds who were in the habit of notching the handles of their whips in the following [5] order:

One before two, three before five
Here one and there one, four alive
Here two and there two and three at the cross
Here one and there one, and Jack at the last.

The notches or tallies ran:

I II III V I I IIII II II IIIX II

It is a far cry from Aberdeenshire to Kent and as the two sets of lines had unmistakably a common origin. I some years later wrote to "*Notes and Queries*" on the subject. Among the replies was one from an Edinburgh correspondent, which is sufficiently curious to merit reproduction:

"A crew of thirty men were taken prisoner, … and their captors determined that half of them should be put to death. Fifteen of them being white and fifteen black, the white captain proposed that the fairest way would be for them to stand in a circle, and that every tenth man should be counted out as a victim till the number was made up. This being agreed to, he arranged them in a few seconds so that all the black men were thrown overboard. Query, how did he manage it? He grouped them according to this formula, which

---

17. The complete title is *Memories of Monquhitter: or Reminiscences of the Early Forties*, and it was an 85-page manuscript published in 1901 by the Banffshire Journal Office, in Banff. Monquhitter is in Aberdeenshire.
18. AB "dote."
19. I can find no meaning for this blurred word.
20. AB "and."

is almost identical with the boys' rhyme:–

> *Two* before one, and *three* before five,
> Here *two*, and there *two*, and *four* go alive
> Then one, and then *one*, and three at a cast
> *One*, two, and *two*, and then Black Jack at last.

... If any reader will arrange fifteen white and fifteen black counters as above, the numbers in italics represents the whites and those in ordinary type the blacks, he will find that by counting onwards and rejecting every tenth piece until fifteen are **6** taken, all the whites will be left. I can offer no opinion either as to the antiquity of the lines or as to how they came to form part of the districts mentioned, but would suggest that the last line in the Aberdeen version:– "And Jenny and her five kye following on fast – is an addition rendered necessary to the bucolic mind by previous mention of 'Jockie." (GSD from Edinburgh in 1878, *Notes and Queries*, p235)

So says Mr. Paterson in his very interesting *Memories of Monquhitter* and his herding days.

A generation has passed away since herding became memory to time of bygone days. And the herd laddies and lassies, with their joys and sorrows, their mystic notches and symbols, are gone forever from Scotland, and will only be known in the ballads and songs of the long, long ago.

Alexander's Father's Early Years

But to return to my narrative. The emancipation of the herd laddie and lassie, was never dreamed of in my father's herding days. He was born August 26th 1791. I remember the Revd. S. Macintosh in preaching his funeral sermon, said he had been born in a remarkable era in history. At the close of the American Revolution, and the beginning of the great French Revolution of 1789, thus living through Britain's terrible struggle when every armed power was against her. For the first fifteen years of the nin[e]teenth century, it was almost continual war with Napoleon, which ended on the field of Waterloo.

A fairly well to do farmer in Buchan, over one hundred years ago, with a large family, however parsimonious, could not bestow larger tochers[21] to his daughters, nor fit his sons with large sums of money to commence business[22] for themselves. Such education as could be obtained at the parish school, time and circumstances considered, to be well di[s]ciplined in the shorter catechism being a cardinal point in home training. Whatever may be said by certain [7] theologians to the contrary, the Shorter Cate-

---

21. This is a Scots term for "dowries."
22. AB "buisness" here and afterwards.

chism[23] is one of the best, if not the very best, compendiums of scriptural truths in our language. Both moral and religious duties strictly inculcated, which has been significant in making the Scot a power at home and revered abroad. Many of the leading men of Britain in Church, State, Army, Navy, and also in the various departments of business have sprung from the rural population of Scotland. The established church and parish schools have been a great boon to Scotland, notwithstanding many defects compared to the new or modern system of education.

My father had left his native parish early in life after his herding days were past, and learned the trade of a shoemaker. This being a lucrative trade at the time, owing to so many young men required into the army, militia and pressed into the navy. It was customary many years ago in rural districts, also in Villages and Towns, for Apprentices to the various trades to get the harvest to themselves to earn a little money. So my father served his time as a (harist heuk[24]) harvest hand with the sic[k]le, which after years came very handy to him shearing among stumps in Canada.

My father was also sometime in Edinburgh working at his trade, but returned to the Town of Peterhead, and began business for himself. He served in the second regiment of the Aberdeenshire local militia during the latter part of the Peninsula war.[25] Was corporal in his company. Married my mother I think in 1820.

Alexander's Mother and Her Father:
Jean Milne Brodie and Captain John Milne

My mother's maiden name was Jean Milne, a common name in Aberdeenshire, and Morayshire, pronounced Mill. In this country often pronounced as Milney. She was born in the town of Elgin Morayshire, and in that ancient royal burgh spent her **8** juvenile[26] years. Her father as far as I have heard, was Captain John Milne, who sailed a merchant vessel from Lossie Mouth. I think he must have been lost at sea, or died when my mother was quite young, as she seldom spoke of him. She used to tell sometimes that he had a very large dog called Neptune, curtailed to Nep, and on his collar was printed, "I'm John Milne's dog. Whose dog are you?" That her father had bought a hen in the market, put it in a basket and sent

---

23. The Shorter Catechism is a series of 107 questions and answers, first written in the 17th century. It is a summary of the beliefs of the traditional Presbyterian Church or Church of Scotland.

24. "Heuk" is an old Scots term for a reaping hook or sickle, and, by extension, the one who does the reaping.

25. The Peninsular War refers to the fight for territory on the Iberian Peninsula, consisting of Portugal and Spain, from 1808 to 1814. In this war Napoleon's French army fought the allied forces of Britain and Spain.

26. AB "juvenal."

Nep home with the hen. She pecked his nose, he swung the basket from side to side and threw the hen out and came home with the empty basket.

The Earl Marischal and Prophesies

My grandmother's maiden name on my mother's side was Jean Davidson, a daughter of the Davidsons of Sarock, a famed farm in the parish of Lonmay in the same district of Buchan. Like the other people mentioned they had been tenants on this farm away back from feudal times. This farm was on Earl Marischal's estate. This good but unfortunate Nobleman raised his retainers and joined the Pretender's standard in 1715, and of course the cause was lost and with it the life and patrimony of many a Scottish nobleman. Earl Marischal escaped to Prussia and became a famous Marshal in the Prussian army. His lands were confiscated and sold. The Sarock family were Episcopalians and out with their Laird in the fi[e]fdom. Branches of the family would not pay their rent only to their ain Laird, emigrated to the plantations in Virginia. In Buchan's *Annals of Peterhead* he tells of Earl Marischal visiting his lost Estates after being exiled for some years, but only made himself known to a few trusty friends. So ended the last Earl of Marischal in Scotland, in Scottish history.

Keith the family name of the Earls of Marischal is of very ancient origin being lost in tradition. The title Marischal comes from [9] the Keiths being for many years Lords Marischal of Scotland. Their principal residence was Inverugie[27] Castle on the banks of the river Uggie about three miles west of Peterhead

> *Raven's Craig* – by Dr. Young,[28] an excerpt
> Where gentle Ugie rolls its stream
> The pebbled bed along
> And kissing soft the winding banks
> The flowery herbs among.[29]

The Pretender, or James the third of England, and James the eighth of Scotland, according to legal descent, that is if he was not a spurious child, as asserted by the Whig party, landed in Peterhead passed the night there, went out to Inverugie Castle and the rebellion of 1715 began. Sir Thomas

---

27. AB "Inveruggie."
28. I was unable to find his full name and birth and death dates.
29. This is just the first stanza of an epic poem that is 38 stanzas long (see Buchan 1819: 50–54).

Learmount, better known as Tamas the Rhymer,[30] prophesied of this Castle. A certain stone was in the upper part of the Castle, in some conspicuous position.

> As long as this stane stan[d]s in the loft[31]
> The name o' Keith sal be aloft
> But whan this stane begins tae fa'a
> The name of Keith sal wear awa.

It is said that according to this prophesy, the stone fell with the Earl's adherence to the Stuarts. History does not state precisely when Tamas the Rhymer lived,[32] but according to allusions made of him by old ballad writers he must have lived at least two hundred years prior to 1715. I have no doubt the house the unfortunate James lodged in is still standing.[33] I could have seen it every day during my childhood had I been so inclined. Whatever might have been its pretentions in 1715 to a Royal abode, one hundred and ninety one years had sadly diminished its appearance among its compeers of the Town. I have seen the Castle of Inverugie when going from Peterhead to St. Fergus. Have looked over **10** the parapet of the bridge down the river as it rolled towards the sea. On the left bank of the river the ruins of Raven's Craig once the proud fortress of the Cheynes. Six hundred years ago its turrets rose majestically from the plain bidding defiance to all who came not in peace. Tamas the Rhymer had certain prophesies regarding the last of the Cheynes[34] and the ruins of this once strong feudal fortress, but I have forgotten the exact words. A hind[35] was to come from the forest and give three bleats and certain stanes were to fa'a. That beneath the hearth stane the tod[36] wid bring her bairns hame [see Back Stories at the end of the chapter].

30. See Back Stories at the end of this chapter. Thomas the Rhymer or Thomas of Learmont was a 13th-century laird who was reputed to have the gift of prophesy. His name and "spiritual gifts" were popularized in the *Ballad of Thomas the Rhymer* (in which he travels to "Elfland," especially through the writing and publishing in three parts of the ballad by Sir Walter Scott (1771–1832).

31. See Back Stories at the end of this chapter for a slightly different version of the same lines.

32. The usual dates given are c. 1220–1298.

33. Inverugie Castle no longer stands. It remains as ruins about three metres above the River Ugie.

34. The Cheynes first owned the land, and the Keiths took over when Mariot Cheyne (who had no brothers to inherit the land) married Edward de Keith in the mid-14th century (see Buchan 1819: 61).

35. This is an old term for a female European deer. It was supposed to be a white hind.

36. AB "toad." Tod refers to a fox in the English of northern England and Scotland.

Tod is the scotch word for fox. Some local poet[37] said of this castle.

Raven's Craig – Dr. Young (an excerpt)
Twas once the pride of yonder plain[38]
The gaze of vulgar eye
But there now rooks and ravens dwell
They run their course and die.

    In the first notes of my narrative I did not mention an episode occasionally told by my Mother when giving us a dressing down as it might be called in Canadian phraseology, but in the Buchan dialect, it was scolding in[39] weathering and sarcastic words, bordering on vituperation. As near as I can recollect it was as follows. That Earl Marischal an ill far'd, ill favoured Sister Jean Keith. So exceedingly ill favoured to look upon that not one of the men of her class could bear the looks of her, notwithstanding her noble blood and illustrious lineage. After the Earl's exile Jean wandered about among her brothers' old tenants with no means of living but the charity of a people devoted to their old Laird. At last Jean found an Asylum with the Sarock family, a member of whom married her, and ill-far'd Jean, like muckle mou'd Meg[40] became an excellent wife and Ancestor of the 11 Davidsons of Sarock. Be this romance or reality, I have told it as I remember hearing it.

    The Sarock family had scattered away from their old home to [a] different part of the world. Just how many there[41] were[42] in the family I am not sure. Know there were[43] John, James, Charles and George being the youngest remained on the farm. John went to France, was in some business in Bordeaux. Do not know what business James followed. When we left Scotland in 1835 he was a very old man living with two unmarried daughters in or near Aberdeen. He was quite wealthy. Have heard my Mother say the Misses Davidson came between her and twenty thousand pounds. Charles was a merchant in Baltimore, State of Maryland for many years. Think he came home to Aberdeen before he died. Have no remembrance of hearing about his family. Have two letters written by him to my grandmother now

---

37. Dr Young in his poem *Raven's Craig*.

38. He has slightly misquoted here. This first line comes from the fourth stanza (Buchan 1819: 54). The first line of the last stanza, from which the rest of the quotation comes, begins with "Tho'".

39. There was an "a" after this word, which would be ungrammatical.

40. The word "muckle" means "big", and this refers to her mouth. For the story of Muckle Mouth Meg, see Back Stories at the end of the chapter.

41. AB "their."

42. AB "was."

43. AB "was."

over one hundred twenty years ago. With the girls of the family I am rather confused. There was Elizabeth, Lizzie, one known as Aunt Percival, never heard her [C[hristian name, and my grandmother as mentioned above. A man by the name of Brown was married to an Aunt of my mother's but whether Lizzie or another called Mary do not know, she was dead before I was born. The name of Mr Brown's farm was Stockbridge. In the common vernacular Stockbrig. Never heard him called any other name but <u>Stocky</u>. His appearance is indelibly stamped on my memory after the laps of three quarters of a century. He was perhaps five feet eight in height, very stout in proportion, large round face, quit[e] rubicund, which indicated that the affairs of the State, Whig or Tory, did not affect his digestion. Of course he was always in his come to town costume when I saw him. Dark corduroy knee pants, low shoes, buff coat with brass buttons, conspicuous in [colour] **[12]** and brightness, a type of the swallow-tailed affinity, the tail wonderfully circumscribed, his waistcoat might have been London Brown with ample pockets, standing up collar open at the breast, at least nine or ten inches displaying a frill or ruffle which stood out in bold relief from his diffusive bosom. A rather low crowned black hat in the crown of which he stored away his bandana when not in use. This representative of a class of farmers, now obsolete in Scotland, was a good man in the full sense of the word, and the world will never see his like again. He often came to our house accompanied by his daughter Betty when in town at the market. My remembrance of Betty is a buxom girl, rather dark red hair, but a face full of smiles. A Jolly Buchan lass of a type as extinct as the Mammoth. Before I was old enough to go to school she often brought me a few sweeties, or a stick of black sugar (licorice[44]) took me on his knee and sang the one song in his memory for it was always the same. I may give something like it phonetically but not the correct orthography:

Oh <u>liss</u> an <u>oh</u> lake fat wi'l I dee.
[Oh ... Will I die]
Ian my bonnie laddie gang tae Lun'un fa'a' me
[Ian my bonnie laddie has gone to London far from me]

Grandmother had lived with my father and mother since they were married. She died either in 1832 or 1833 (I am not sure of the date) aged eighty four years and some months. Aunt Percival had lived in England many years, had forgotten her native dialect, was quite different in manner and speech from the Peterhead people. Can remember her as being taller than my grandmother, think she was older and exercised the prerogative in no measured terms. Her husband had been deceased many years. Have a dim recollection of hearing he was a ship Captain and lost at sea. She had

---

44. AB "liquorace."

[13] a son, Captain John Percival, also lost at sea, think he never came to Peterhead, at least I have no remembrance of hearing of it. May have been before I was born. Whatever had been the circumstances of her husband and son, she was well provided for financially, as she bequeathed nice legacies to her relations at her death. Which I think occurred in 1830. Can remember being at her house with my mother. Everything was in tosh[45] order. Whether I had touched something tabooed, which elicited a lecture on obedience and the proper bringing up of children, and the general delineation of all things Mundane, was given with significant glances darted at me, I was somewhat daunted but felt innocent in doing anything to call forth such a lecture. She kept a maid who had to toe the mark every time or she would suffer a generally severe tong[u]e lashing. My mother had two sisters, Charlotte and Mary. Knew that Charlotte was older than my mother that she died a bride, that my mother always spoke of her as a young woman of more than ordinary ability and was greatly lamented by a large circle [of] relations and friends. I do not know whether Mary was older or younger than my mother, think she was younger and died when a child, as she seldom spoke of her as she did of Charlotte.

My mother in speaking of her Uncle George, called him Sawk, that being the local pronunciation of Sarock. He was much younger than my grandmother quite active in 1835. He had only three of a family that I ever heard of, James, Charles and Eliza. James died in Indian from the sting of a scorpion before I was born. Charles I never saw. Eliza I have seen a few times. She was Mrs Hutton, was at her home a few times with my mother at Invernetty Mills a few miles from Peterhead. [14] Remember three of a family Eliza, George and James. James died from the effects of falling on a caldron of boiling water before we left Peterhead. George and Eliza came to the same school as we did, but having a long walk did not attend very regular. From a letter my mother received from her Uncle James he told of Mr Hutton's bankruptcy, and had left the place. So far as I can remember there was a tone of pity with a tinge of resentment in his letter about the family. Think from innuendos that Eliza's marriage had not been approved of by the family and kindred. She was a famed beauty, and the one maiden of the famed farm of Sarock, and was expected to do something meritorious in the matrimonial market. Judging from what I have heard, John Hutton was a good kind husband and father but like many more men in business, he speculated too far, without sufficient capital and the result was disastrous. Eliza Hutton was a famed beauty like her mother, was to be educated as a young lady suitable for a <u>Coronet</u>, had not the vain desire of riches allured her father too far. To use a sea phrase, he carried too much sail for his ballast. In my grand Uncle's letter to my mother his regret seemed to be for the young girl, whose education had not been commensurate with their means

---

45. Scots dialect form for "neat" or "tidy."

of now making a living. So the Huttons passed away from our ken, likely forever. Such is the way of the world. We are all John Tamson's bairns,[46] but where are we.

My grandmother Milne managed to give her two daughters a good education, not often the case among the common people in Buchan over a hundred years ago. Just what age the girls were when they moved from Elgin to Peterhead I never heard. Know [15] that they both attended Mr Imiries School in Peterhead. Mr. Imirie was a famous teacher of young men and girls in the higher branches of education in his day. My mother taught a class of boys prepatory to going to the parish school. Also a class of girls, particularly in sewing [k]nitting, sampler work, all kinds of needle work considered necessary for a girl to be proficient in previous to becoming a matron in the good old Town of Peterhead. A bride was thought of little account if she could not make her own gown, the bridegroom's shirt, and all her own fabulaws.[47] There were no[48] sewing machines in those days to bib and tucker, half a century had to pass into history before Mr. Singer had patented his renowned machine.

Back Stories of Chapter One

Family Tree
Father's Side

Alexander Brodie—Barbara Anderson Brodie

Anne, Jean Elizabeth, Mary Margaret Isabella, Alexander George, William James

Mother's Side

Jean Davidson Milne* = John, James, Charles, **George, Elizabeth, Aunt Percival and Mary

(JDM)* Jean Milne Brodie = Charlotte and Mary

(GM)** James, Charles, Eliza Hutton***

(EH)***Eliza, George, James

Thomas the Rhymer

Thomas the Rhymer or Thomas of Learmont was a 13th-century laird (c. 1220–1298) who was reputed to have the gift of prophesy. His name and "spiritual gifts" were popularized in the *Ballad of Thomas the Rhymer* which included a part in which he travelled to "Elfland." Thomas the

---

46. This is a Scottish phrase that means we are all equal, that we are all God's children. See Back Stories in this chapter.

47. I haven't been able to find a specific meaning for this, but I feel that it probably refers to various items of her clothing.

48. AB "was now."

Rhymer became well-known to literature-loving Scots such as Uncle Alex in the 19th century through the writing and publication in three parts of the ballad by Sir Walter Scott (1771–1832).

The prophecy concerning the fox and her "bairns" is recorded by Ferguson in poem form including the following lines:

> Ugie, Ugie, by the sea,
> Lairdless shall they lands be;
> And beneath thy ha' hearth stane,
> The tod shall bring her bairns home.
> (Ferguson 1881: 115)

Peter Buchan records the relationship between the stone and the house of Keith as follows:

> As lang's this stane stands on the craft
> The name o' Keith shall be alaft
> But when it begins to fa'
> The name o' Keith shall wear awa'.
> (Buchan 1819: 64)

Muckle-Mouth Meg

The story of Muckle-Mouth Meg is about Lady Agnes Murray, one of the daughters of Sir Gideon Murray. His family and another Borders family, the Scotts, were competing with each other. Young William Scott is said to have raided the castle of the Murrays, for which Gideon was going to punish him by hanging. Lady Agnes was famously unattractive, with a large mouth and jaw said to dominate her face. She offered marriage to her as an alternative to hanging. William turned her down, but when he saw the rope that was to hang him, and saw Lady Agnes' sorrow at his impending execution, he decided to marry her, or so the story goes. The poet Robert Browning (1812–89) wrote a poem that took the story a slightly different direction (but with the same result).

We are All John Tamson's Bairns

Dr. Joseph Roy, born in 1841 in Glasgow, wrote a song by this name. The chorus of the song runs as follows:

> O' we're a' John Tamson's bairns,
> We're a' John Tamson's bairns,
> There ne'er will be peace till the world again
> Has learned to sing wi' micht and main
> We're a' John Tamson's bairns.

You can find the full poem on this website: www.rampantscotland.com/songs/blsongs_tamson.htm. According to this same source, John Tamson was said to come from Aberdeenshire.

Chapter Two
Life in Peterhead

Just what money my father and mother had saved prior to their marriage I never heard. About 1829 or thirty they purchased a property in the Longate[49] (Better known by Langate) consisting of a good large house, shop, and what might by some [be] called a parlour, but in our parlance it was simply ben[50] the house and we the bairns only got admittance on rare occasions. Upstairs there[51] was accommodation for two families; have no remembrance of the upstairs rooms being without tenants.[52] On one side of the garden but attached to the back part of the house fronting the street was a long low building which was divided into kitchen, washing house, a place [for] peats and coal, and a mangle[53] house. Grandmother[54] ran the mangle[55] as long as she was alive and well. At the end of the garden but fronting the street. One was occupied by a Mrs. Alexander, better known by the sobriquet of the wiffie[56] (Ilshmer). The other tenant was Bell Massie. What rent they paid I never heard. Mrs Alexander rented a garden away somewhere about the environs[57] of the town. Herself and boy managed the garden raised onions, cabbages, leeks and [15A] potatoes and sold them in the market. Whether this constituted all their means of living I do not know. There was an older son a weaver who drove a loom in a large weaving shop. Some untoward accident had caused him to walk with giving one leg a kind of spasmodic jerk which gave him the sobriquet of Stumpy Georgie Ilshiner [?].

Bell's business so far as I know was teasing and trying to retail milk supplied to her by someone near the Town that kept a cow or two. She came one day and in pressing terms solicited my mother's patronage for the sale of her milk, that it was not fair to go to any other woman for milk when she a tenant was in the milk business. My mother admitted the justice of her plea. So accordingly next morning I was instructed to go to Bell's next morning for milk, to the breakfast porridge. I entered Bell's

---

49. See Back Stories in this chapter.

50. "Ben" is a Scottish term that means "inside" in reference to a house. It traditionally referred to the fancy inner room or parlour of a small house.

51. AB "their."

52. AB "tennants" here and elsewhere.

53. This is a British term for a wringer washer.

54. This would be Jean Davidson Milne.

55. AB "mangel."

56. This is a Scottish term for an old woman.

57. AB "invirons."

house with many misgivings, for we know well Bell was no sanitary[58] scientist. Her house had a strong odour of oakum,[59] the ledge[60] of her window where she kept and measured her milk was far from improved dairy style.[61] In the upper part of the small window was stretched from on[e] corner to the other cobwebs, like a gauze frieze, and many an unsuspecting fly became a feast to the unmerciful spider. Bell herself was not an attractive person. Nature had been very ungenerous toward her in all its multifarious aspects. She was a termagant[62] of the first water. In fact a kind of Arab on a small scale. If she did not hate everyone, she had little love to anyone, and no one appeared to fraternize with her. During my life occasionally, when in a kind of reverie, or reflective mood, reminiscences of Bell have come before my mind's eye, and the very thought of a person who befriended no one and had not a single friend, or relation on earth to bestow her tithe of kindness towards them, is a position so sad, so bereft of [16] [the] image [of] righteousness that we shudder to think of such a life. A person may have a very uncouth physic, coarse features, tout ensemble tos lang sing yet have an enviable disposition that qualifies all defects, a mind so stored with good gifts that the untoward physical are gone. But poor Bell had no redeeming quality whatever that I ever heard of. Of course boys would play tricks on her, and her fury would burst forth in demoniac passion. A few young lads one summer gloaming[63] were sporting in our back yard. Whether they had exhausted their mission on one kind of sport or whether they thought a change in the program would be in improvement to the evening's amusement never was told. At all events it was proposed to put a sod on the top of Bell's lum[64] and smoke her out of her house. The sod was not a common grass sod but the tough surface of the moss cut off before coming to the proper peat. The sod was generally put at the back of the fire and burned slow. The sod was soon procured. The tallest boy stooped down and another one with the sod mounted his back, and as the tall lad rose erect, the other gained his shoulders. It was easy then to ascend the roof, the eaves not being higher than a tall man's head. The sod was placed securely on the top of Bell's lum. The boy down again, then an

---

58. AB "sanitary."

59. Oakum is fibre (typically traditionally hemp or jute) infused with tar, and then used for caulking or packing the joints of timbers in wooden boats.

60. AB "leget."

61. Pasteurization, the process using heat to make milk sanitary and safe for consumption was invented by Louis Pasteur in 1864.

62. This term was first used by medieval Christians to refer to a god they mistakenly believed that Muslims worshipped. It came to refer to an individual who is overbearing and quarrelsome.

63. The period of twilight or dusk before the dark of night takes over.

64. Scottish dialect term for "chimney."

instant skedaddle to the street corner to witness the effect, and Bell's wrath. Sometimes boys' tricks begin in comedy, but end almost in tragedy. Bell had for once sweeped up her peat mess and thrown the dust, and small particles of peat on her evening's fire. In a few minutes her little house was full of smoke, and having no other vent, the door was evacuating[65] smoke in clouds rising slowly and wholly obscuring her house. She was out on the street roaring out lum a low, lum a low[66] in vociferous tones. In a few minutes there was a crowd, pails, and buckets were shortly on hand and the men [?] [17] well laid contribution. Geordie thinking the fun had assumed a rather too serious aspect, whispered the cause to Tam Stuart who entered the front door and ran round to the back of Bell's house, and lifting James to the root who threw down the sod, which Tam quickly deposited in the midden. But Bell was nowise reconciled. It was the loons[67] (meaning us boys) and that ner do weil Tam Stuart that had caused all the trouble. She vowed venge[a]nce on every boy on the street, and to add fuel to her fury the boys on the street shouted

> Bonnie Bellie Massie, wis ance a bonnie lassie
> But now she's lien tae ewakin[68] teasing mucle oakum

But to return to Bell's milk and the morning's porridge. Her milk was not only odour[ou]s of oakum but tasted strongly of tar. Neither bribes of sugar, treacle, coaxing, starving, angry threats of dire punishment of spanking galore, could induce one spoonful of porridge to go over our throats accompanied with Bell's milk. The result was that I was sent next morning to our old and trusty milk woman Kirsty Dinnis. Bell espied me returning from Kristy's with my flagon of milk. She accosted me in very unsavory language why I had gone to Kirsty's instead [of] coming to her as agreed upon yesterday morning. The only defence I could make was the truth. Your milk is not good. It smells of oakum and tastes of tar. If ever a boy got a calling down I did. One of the many ill names launched at me was an ill bred geet[69]. I did not know the meaning of half her words. Her de-

---

65. AB "evacuanting."

66. I have been unable to find a meaning for "a low" here. It might just mean "on fire."

67. "Loon" is a Scots term for "boy" or "young man."

68. I can't discover what this means, but the "tae" is probably "to" and the "lien" is probably a word that in standard English would end with *-ing-*. The same is possibly true of the last word. The phrase probably has something to do with the effects of working with a lot of oakum.

69. This is the old Scots pronunciation of the mildly insulting word that in British English is usually spelled and pronounced as "git."

livery was fast and furious. I believe the most eloquent Billingsgate[70] orator would only have been a neophyte to her. She went straight to my mother then ensued a fierce but undecided combat. Bell failed in convincing my mother that her milk was immune from oakum taint or any alloy whatever, and my mother signally failed in convincing [18] Bell to the contrary. In pugilistic phraseology it was a draw.

The garden was divided into two parts, the flower garden and the kale[71] yard. The flower garden was located so that it would receive the largest amount of sunshine possible. A wall or dike perhaps ten or twelve feet high sheltered it from the northeast wind. Along this wall was planted a few apple and pear trees their branches fastened up to the wall, in a spreading position. Between the gardens was a bleach green[72] seemingly a necessity in Scotland many years ago.

I think the people of Peterhead had a great love of flowers. All who had a bit of backyard, and most residents had a favoured spot specially devoted to flowers.

I am not florist enough to know the names of the many beautiful flowers that adorn the lawns and windows of both rural and urban dwellings of Ontario. But I see few of the beauties there common in well kept gardens in Peterhead seventy five years ago. Many beautiful flowers from foreign countries have been acclimatized since 1835 now quite common. The principal beauties I remember were in early spring, almost among the snow were the crocus, snow-drop, then carnations, sweet Williams, [and] wall flowers. July flowers, peonies,[73] lilies,[74] a gorgeous flower called the tiger lily. Tulips seemed to be a particular favourite and the more variegated[75] flowers in a group, the more esteemed. A shade was often placed over a more than ordinary beautiful specimen to protect it from the sun in order to retain the full bloom longer. We had a large showy red flower in our garden called the scarlet tomentossa.[76] My father bought it from a man that raised flowers to sale. It grew at least three feet high put out branches about a foot from the ground to the top, on each branch a flower. Do not

70. Billingsgate, one of the wards of London, is used in this reference to the stereotypically foul language used by vendors in the fish market there that was established in 1699.

71. AB "kail." This is a Scots term for vegetable garden, not just for the growing of kale.

72. This refers to a place where laundry was done, and wet laundry was hung up to dry.

73. AB "peonys."

74. AB "lilys."

75. AB "varigated."

76. The species name *tomentossa* appears a number of times for a great variety of plants, shrubs and trees. It refers to a plant with woolly plant "hairs." The English derivative is "tomentose." Peterhead being a shipping centre, the Scots there had access to plants from all over the world. The plant might even have been the red-blossomed *Sesbania tomentosa* of Hawaii.

know whether it was an annual, biannual,[77] a perennial[78] **[19]** [and I] have never seen another of the same kind since. There was the ubiquitous marigold, and the many sweet smelling accessories[79] to a flower garden having no pretentions to beauty of flower, still requisite to a well arranged flower garden.

What the property above mentioned would have realized in 1835 I have no remembrance I ever heard. I think however not near so much as the same size of lot and quality of buildings would realize in a Canadian town of the same population.

Back Stories of Chapter Two

Longate in 1981

It was with great excitement in 1981 that I approached Longate in Peterhead, the street upon which my Brodie ancestors lived. I knew that it was highly unlikely that their house would still be standing, but it was still magic to be there on that street. I saw it during the heady days of the North Sea oil boom in Scotland. I saw a lot of men wearing cowboy hats, something I know that Uncle Alex would have been fascinated by. On Longate I saw one such man, at least in his forties, with a very exotically dressed young lady on a Saturday morning. Uncle Alex would doubtless have noticed and commented on it as well. I think he would have agreed with me that she was probably a "lady of the evening."

Longate is one of the most easterly of the streets in contemporary Peterhead, running roughly north and south. It is one road west of Seagate, which faces a part of the North Sea mostly enclosed by a peninsula. It connects to the south to Peterhead Bay. Longate itself is only a few minutes' walk from the sea. The Brodies would have heard and smelled the sea every day they lived there.

In 1877, according to *Worrall's Directory of the Northeastern Counties of Scotland*, there were six boot and shoe makers living on Longate, as well as other small businesses (1877: 465), so it probably would not have looked or smelled strange to Uncle Alex.

What I saw in 1981 was a mixture of houses, lots of flats, and businesses, none of them related to footwear. But it was still where part of my family came from.

77. AB "byannual."

78. AB "perannual."

79. AB "accessarys."

Chapter Three
Planning and Preparing to Leave

Notwithstanding a comfortable house and a fair way of making a living, my father had never been reconciled wholly to the shoemaking and leather merchants, as supplying leather to other shoemakers from a wholesale firm in Aberdeen, as a mean[s] of living to old age. In a Seaport Town where the loss of a vessel or the failure of a fishing season meant many pounds to be raised from the debit side of the ledger, [it] was often the cause of much loss and disappointment. As time passed on and the family increased, it was easy to apprehend that a separation[80] was inevitable in the near future. Although there were many trades and occupations for well educated young men abroad in the world, the main [o]utlet for Peterhead boys was the Sea, the Colonies or foreign service. The prosperity of the Town depended almost wholly on the shipping interest hence the popularity of boys cho[o]sing a seafaring life. But to be bound an apprentice for four or five years to a whaling vessel, bound from Peterhead to Greenland, Davis Strait, perhaps Hong Kong or Calcutta. Owing to stormy seas and inhospitable climates, meant separation little short of death itself. If a Greenland whaler was successful and returned [20] full ship in June or first two weeks of July, she frequently went a voyage up the Baltic to Dantzig[81], Riga, St. Petersburg, and sometimes round North Cape to Archangel. This made a winter's voyage and was much dreaded.

As days passed into weeks and weeks into months, my father and mother cherishing a strong desire to keep their family together as long as possible, determined to go to America. It was all America in those days. Canada was seldom used in Scottish phraseology, only to distinguish Upper, from Lower Canada. A longing for a more active life as larger freeholder, and farmer in Upper Canada, then considered an [E]lysium[82] to dwell in, grew from a kind of romance to a stern reality. During the winter of 1834 my father seemed to [be] less assiduous in business than usual, and more prone to collecting outstanding accounts, which amounted to about £300. Many of those debts were of long standing. A few paid a little, or gave a little on account. One man gave his pick on an account, of £5. A twenty five dollar pick. About $1,150.00 was left with a Lawyer to collect when we left Peterhead. I am sorry to tell, not one cent of this money was ever recovered. Letters passed back and fore, for several years about it. Many reasons being assigned for not paying. Being mostly seafaring men, some had left

---

80. AB "seperation."
81. AB "Dantzic."
82. Elysium was a concept of the afterlife as developed in ancient Greek religion and philosophy.

the place, others had been reduced to extreme poverty by the almost complete failure of whale fishing. Out of the whole sum not to recover even one five pound was rather suspicious looking. There was no lack of excuses, some no doubt were dead. Others had left the place and poverty had also played its part. But Peterhead people had certain doubts as to the Lawyer's probity. Had this money been forthcoming, as was expected it would have made a very great difference to our [21] circumstances in the future.

By the end of 1834 it [was] a foregone conclusion that we were preparing to cross the great Atlantic Ocean. In the long winter evenings of 1835, my father often gathered us all around the Kitchen fire, and read from pamphlets circulated no doubt by land speculators to encourage emigration. There were very glowing accounts of the country in these pamphlets. Its great resources. Its unparall[el]ed beauty of landscape, along the great rivers and lakes, teeming with fish, especially salmon.[83] The woods alive with deer, wild turkeys, and the smaller game birds in numberless flocks. So to live, sum[p]tuously every day, was simply a matter of course. Occasionally a neighbor or two would call in to spend the evening, and di[s]cuss the grandeur of American scenery and the freedom of man's will.

On one of those occasions a prominent Tailor of the Town, James Reid, being present, a map of Upper Canada was spread on the table, and James becam[e] enthusiastic in praise of the country around Lake Simcoe.[84] James although confined to the bench, and lapboard of a tailor's shop, had a natural inclination towards being a Nimrod.[85] He expatiated in elegant language on the pleasures of bear hunting. And the different kinds of game abounding in the great forest primeval. No game laws. No restrictions whatever to the will of man. Go ye and possess the land. <u>Quantum libet</u>.[86]

The first winter we were in Canada was a very severe one.[87] The ground froze up on the tenth of November, and the snow fell a few days after. There was no thaw, the people spoke of the January thaw, but it never came. The bare ground was not [22] seen until the first of May. Our log house was a very cold one of its kind. Its roof being not to see one of the most primitive of fashion, though not as good to exclude the weather, the rigours of which we had no idea. Every thing froze, the bread so hard as to [be] hacked off the loaf with an axe, and then thawed at the fire. It was not very palatable after this process. At breakfast one morning my mother's tea spoon froze to the cup, and the cup to the saucer, all lifted together by the spoon. This

---

83. See the Back Stories section in this chapter ("Teeming with Fish").

84. A good number of Scottish emigrants of that time ended up in that area.

85. Nimrod was a king in the Middle East referred to the in the Bible. Over time he came to be associated with hunting and generally living off the land.

86. AB "Quantam libet." This is a Latin phrase that can be translated as "as much as you like" or "as great as you please."

87. See Back Stories in this chapter ("The Cold Winter of 1835–6").

incident recalled to her mind James Reid's laudatory on the beauties of the Lake Simcoe district. She laughed heartily and said, "O' I wish Jamie Reid was on the borders of Lake Simcoe this morning."

I have rather digressed from the trend of my story, but I wish to point out the different in describing the country or place from the different points of view of visitors. The motives for description may vary according to impressions of interest and the id[i]osyncrasy of the individual. The truth may be told by each observer, yet the whole truth may not be manifest. The fact that in winter, in the most farmed parts of Ontario, the mercury falls to from ten to twenty degrees below zero, occasionally, and in summer rises to one hundred in the shade. This is an anomaly only experience can reconcile. That the finest qualities of peaches, grapes and other fruit peculiar to the more genial climates of Europe, thrive to perfection in a climate where the extremes of temperature are so great, is certainly paradoxical. James Reid had no idea of the extremes of temperature that often prevail in the townships bordering on Lake Simcoe, or he might have qualified his panegyric on the perfections of the Simcoe district.

By the beginning of March it was no longer a probability but a [23] decided understanding, that we were to sail early in April. Four families from the same town, and parish, besides our own, also four unmarried men, and two girls under my father's care. Those families were well known to each other, which conduced much to the harmony that prevailed during the voyage. They had consulted whether they would said from Peterhead or Aberdeen. There were the Hendersons, Stuarts, Galloways, a Mrs Mackie and family going to meet her husband somewhere in Lower Canada. Our own family, David Sinclair, Alexander Morrison, John Macgillivray going to an Uncle in Whitby, James Browns, Betty our cousin and Helen Miller, a kind of ward of my father's.

Our home and all its appurtenances were sold to a young merchant Alexander Birnie, then followed the group Auction. All the furniture was sold. In face everything that could not be packed into boxes except the cradle, that had rocked us all. It came to Canada and did excellent service, being borrowed around in the neighborhood to rock the first baby in many families, as it [was] considered bad luck to rock the first baby in a new cradle. I have no distinct recollection of great sorrows or regret at parting with cherished things that had been familiar to my childhood associations since memory's dawn. I was at school and in my class the day before we sailed. With most of my classmates the parting salutations were brief. "We'el gaeu tae America Alick. I'se be there some day." My favorite Chum Davie Robertson and I were sorry to part, the only case in which tears were shed, but our grief was greatly mitigated by a mutual understanding that Davie would certainly come to America sometime, and although many years might intervene he would know me by the mark of a large cut on the back of my left hand, and I would know by a scar [24] on his forehead from the kick of a horse.

Well after the lapse of fifteen years, Davie came to America. Our juvenile ideas of America were vague. We had no idea that we could be in America and still as far apart as the wide Atlantic. He was engaged as a book[k]eeper to a large land speculating Company in the western States head quarters Chicago.[88] He got leave to go home and visit the first world's Exhibition in London. Called to see a friend in Toronto on his way, had only one day to spare to come and see me, and that day was Sunday. His friend failed to get a livery rig in time to drive twenty five miles and back again and allow him time to reach the Steamer in time for sailing from New York. Have heard he came back to Chicago, was in the Company's employ until it became bankrupt. So exit Davie from my ken.

An Incident Concerning Boarding

A rather curious incident occurred to us three elder boys a few evening previous to sailing. Just as we were getting into bed a loud knock on the front door caused us to delay undressing. Jamie went and opened the door, the man ran back to the other side of the street. Jamie reported his strange conduct to my father who showed no sign of anything being amiss but immediately[89] went outside as if there was some important business on hand. Next morning a number of boxes were arranged in the back yard, and the oldest son of the Stuart family, Willie, busy painting the name William Wilson (with his finger) in white paint on them. Subsequent events cleared up this Ignis Fatuus.[90] Alexander Stuart was a house carpenter, he was terribly in debt. He promised my father and James Galloway that if they would assist him to [25] get away to America he would pay every bawbee[91] of his debt with the first money he and family would earn. "So help me God" and confer on him and family a never to be forgotten kindness. Believing the man to be sincere after such protestations to honesty pay his debt, they did help him at the risk of being caught in a fraudulent act. With the aid of the Captain of the ship we were to sail in, they succeeded in getting his tool chest and many other things from the shop, which of course was rented and the rent unpaid, at night, aboard the ship as she lay at the pier. Notwithstanding that the officers of the law were watching every movement of the fame as they thought, the Captain stowed him away in some dark secret hole under the cabin from which he emerged from his

---

88. AB "Chigago," both times.

89. AB "immeadiately" here and elsewhere.

90. Latin, literally translated as "fire foolish," referring to a will-of-the-wisp, marsh gas igniting and providing brief flashes of light. More metaphorically it refers to something deceptive or hard to find or catch.

91. An early Scottish coin of low value, a Scottish half-penny.

larva state, the second day after sailing into the original man Stuart. When he made his appearance on deck his clothes adorned with shavings, he certainly was a Rara avis[22] to the juvenile part of the passengers. Someone asked him if he had been cold, he shrugged his shoulders and said "maist D... h. Although young and old of the passenger knew well that a Double entendre was being played none but my father and James Galloway and the Captain knew the true state of affairs. I am sorry to tell that his man never paid one cent of his debt, though him and his sons earned large wages in Toronto, saved money, and bought land in the Township of Beverl[e]y.[93] It seemed the cons[ta]bles could not seize his belongings under the name of William Wilson, nor prevent his family from coming aboard the ship. They could do nothing unless they could arrest him, and in this they were fairly baffled. As a matter of course the passengers and the people fathered on the pier, wonders what the eclairicis[s]ement[94] would be, when they saw his family on board, his creditors [26] seeing his boxes going down the hatch and knew well there was a trick to undo in the near future.

Our family consisted of five boys and one girl. In order as follows, George, James, Alexander A., Jean, William, Charles John about nine months old.

Back Stories of Chapter Three

Whaling in Peterhead

The period of whaling in Peterhead stretched from the first ship sent out to Greenland in 1788, to the last ship that sailed in 1893. By the 1820s, the Greenland whales had been over-hunted so the ships took further chances by going to and through the Davis Strait to Baffin Island. One disastrous year in 1830 may have started the Brodie parents thinking that there needed to be a different career path for their boys.

In 1830, the "wrecking year," no fewer than 31 ships from the British fleet of 91 were lost at Davis Strait. Many more returned "clean" (no cargo), each with its own dreadful tale to tell. It was commonplace for ships to become "beset" in the ice floes for days or even weeks on end, but the season of 1830 was the worst ever seen. Returning captains reported cases of severe frostbite, scurvy, madness and death (Sutherland, "The Peterhead Whalers, 1788-1893," www.nefa.net/archive/peopleandlife/sea/pheadwhalers.htm).

92. Latin for "rare bird," referring to a strange sight.

93. Beverley Township was founded in 1792, and has since been incorporated into the community of Flamborough (or Flamboro) in the city of Hamilton.

94. French term for which the direct translation is "clarification," referring to an explanation that sheds light on something that has been obscure or not understood.

John Steckley
The Cold Winter of 1835-6

The winter of 1835–6 was unusually cold. Lorin Blodget (1823–1901), who can be said to be the founder of climatology in the United States, said the following:

> At Toronto, Captain Lefroy found the months of winter, 1835–6, the coldest of the period from 1830 to 1854, the mean of this period for 23 years being 29°.9 [−1.167 degrees C.], and that of 1835–6, 26°.3 [−3.167 degrees C.]. It is said to have been the most severe in North America since 1779–80 (Can. Jour. Sci., &c) (Blodget 1857: 151).

The Captain Lefroy mentioned was John Henry Lefroy (1817–1890), a military officer/colonial administrator/scientist, who lived in Toronto from 1842 to 1853, running the newly (1839) established Toronto Magnetic and Meteorological Observatory, created by Edward Sapine (1788–1883), also an officer/scientist. The observatory is located in the main St. George campus of the University of Toronto.

The Travellers

Five Families
1. Brodies
2. Hendersons
3. Stuarts
4. Galloways
5. Mackies

Individuals
David Sinclair
Alexander Morrison
John MacGillivray
James Brown
Betty (Brodie cousin)
Helen Miller (ward)

The Stuarts

The Hamilton directory for 1867–8 listed several Stuarts, including a "city collector," a clerk, a bookkeeper, a "city wood and hay inspector" and James Stuart and Co., a successful wholesale wine and liquor merchant that put an ad in the directory (*Sutherland's City of Hamilton and County of Wentworth Directory for 1867-8*, James Sutherland, compiler, Ottawa: Hunter Rose and Company [Static.torontopubliclibrary.ca/da/pdfs/37131055372742d.pdf].

Teeming with Fish

A good example of the type of promotional material encouraging British people to emigrate to Canada is *Emigration, the advantages of emigration to Canada, the substance of two lectures*, published in 1831 by the English writer William Cattermole. The following is what he had to say about the fish in Canada:

> The lakes teem with white fish, salmon, trout, sturgeons, musquenonge, white and black bass, pickerill [pickerel], eels, and herrings in vast quantities, salmon and white fish are delicious, particularly the latter, I know no fish in Britain that surpasses it ..." (https://archive.org/stream/emigrationadvan00cattgoog/emigrationadvan00cattgoog-djvu.txt).

Chapter Four
Crossing the Atlantic on the *Alert*

We sailed from the town of Peterhead on the third day of April 1835 in the Brig Alert bound for Quebec. A large crowd had gathered at the two piers as she sailed from the south harbour to bid adieu to relations and dear friends they would never see again. There was much farewelling and shedding of tears. Sobs as if hearts would burst asunder and amid this sorrow were being pledged solemn vows of writing immediately[95] on arrival at Quebec. The owner of the brig, James Hogg, or in the Peterhead vernacular mad Jamie Hogg[96] being subject to certain whims of mind causing him to have his own way in spite of law or custom. Had on some previous voyages to Quebec refused to receive a pilot onboard. Said he knew the way to Quebec as well as any pilot. The result of this obstinate[97] and unreasonable conduct he could not get a crew to sail with him. He was an old sailor, and of the old school. His knowledge of the world apart from navigation and the practical part of managing a ship was meagre indeed. He had been very successful as a whaler in his young days. Was wealthy, lived in a grand house, and unmarried. He stood on the pier and gave orders to the sailors as the cable was cast loose, and the brig moved away from the pier, and when the last cheer died away he called out in stentorian voice, "God be with you all." [27] Wheeled about and marched up the pier without turning his head around again.

That peculiar motion of a sailing vessel even in a comparatively calm sea soon causes sickness. As the brig cleared the harbour into the bay, the commotion between decks was confusion in all its most pitiable, and ludicrous aspects. Human nature in its multifarious phases was signally exhibited. Some were of a praising, some scolding about getting their bedding stowed away into their allotted berths. Some of the men driven to the last limit of their patience, were expressing their troubles in words not quite in conformity with the third commandment. Mothers at their wits end, while children hung around them in doleful yammer. Mothers and children parting in violent spasms with their last repast in the land of their forefathers. There was such confusion and such an extraordinary kind of it, that it seemed impossible things would ever come right again. A few young men and girls thought to ward off sickness by waking from stern to stem, as if a prize was to be awarded to the best pedestrian. They seemed determined to defraud old Daddie Neptune of his customary obeisance exacted from all who have not yet been rocked in his cradle but they had

---

95. AB "immeadiately" (here and elsewhere).

96. See Back Stories in this chapter.

97. AB "obistinate."

to succumb to the inevitable, and run to the side of the ship and part with the evidences of hospitality of dear friends they would never enjoy again in much distress. While the sailors on duty berated in no dialect tones, <u>Go to the lee side you lubbers</u>. It is very seldom that a sailing vessel has the wind so fair that there is not a lee side. If the win[d] is even so slightly one direction, she will lean over from the wind, the low side is the lee, the high side the weather. This is in contradistinction to larboard [28], and starboard. Looking from the stern to the low starboard is on the right and larboard is on the left, no matter how the wind blows.

The brig tacked in the bay during the afternoon waiting for a cabin passenger from Aberdeen who turned up in the evening. Anchored during the night. No doubt I slept so sound that I have no remembrance of any complaints or commotion on this our first night on the ocean.

The final farewell was on Saturday morning. Friends had risen early and walked to a point of land as near the ship as possible as she rounded the co[a]st northward, and gave their last salute, by waving handkerchiefs and a swinging of hats, which was answered from the ship by the same token and three hearty cheers from the sailors, and away we sailed leaving Peterhead on the larboard lee. Sunday was a beautiful day, not a cloud to dim the horizon. Nearly everyone had recovered from sickness as come on deck, as this was likely to be the last sight of the "land of blue mountains high covered north [?]" to all passengers. As we entered the Pentland [F]irth, Duncans by head and John O'Groats House on the larboard, while away to the north rose the Orkneys black and bare to appearance in the great expanse of water. No wonder the Roman sailors thought they had reached the <u>Ultima Thule</u>,[98] if the Islands appeared to them as uninviting two thousand years ago as they did to my boyish view in 1835. Away in the distant south glistened brightly in the evening's sunset snow on the hills of Caithness. Beautiful as the day had been to a landsman's eye, the sailors said the sunset sky presaged a storm. We had now entered the great Atlantic, the [29] Captain said he knew by the great swell of the waves by the German Ocean. As the evening closed over the ocean the glimmering lights of the lighthouse of Cape Wrath sank below the horizon and Caledonia became a memorial of the past to all the passengers except one.

During Sunday night or early Monday morning the presaged storm broke forth in terrific violence, and for three days and three nights the brig was tossed as a mere toy on the great sweeping billows of the western ocean. The lurches and giddy motion of the vessel brought on sickness again more severe than ever, and the half deck (as it was called) was a scene, could it

---

98. The term "Ultima Thule" has been used since at least the first century B.C. and the days of the Roman poet Virgil (70–19 B.C.) to refer to a far-off land, particularly in the north, and symbolically as an unattainable goal. In later centuries it became associated with Norway, Iceland and Greenland.

have been seen in the light of day away beyond my knowledge of vocables to describe. Shrieks, prayers, recriminations so uncouth as to border on blasphemy. While every great lurch from larboard to starboard, someone groaned in sepulchral quavers down we go, but we did no go down. Sometime in the night or early morning the Mate came down and hung a canteen on the mast. It rolled around the mast giving ghastly glimmer, making the scene more weird than total darkness.

The tin dishes procured by the passengers for culinary purposes being of many shapes, sizes and intentions, were hung up where a nail could be driven. They ringled, and tingled and anon gave a solemn peal as dirge to our burial [?] in the "deep deep see." But amid all this commotion and apparent danger children slept in the arms of old Morpheus, unheeding of danger until a huge wave rolled the brig almost on her beam ends and threw them from their berths on the half decks.

Day light came at last but little of it entered this circumscribed **30** abode of over forty human beings. Two disks of thick glass eight or ten inches in diameter inserted in the deck on each side, was all the access of light except what came down the hatch, which to be closed during storms to prevent water rushing down when a heavy sea swept the deck. Ventilation and sanitary science had no part in the equipment of a passenger ship in 1835, at least not in the *Alert*. The great storm had not damaged the ship very much. The half of the larboard bulwarks were carried away and the spanker boom fell on the dock with a crash but was not washed overboard.

We had several severe storms during the voyage but this first one was undoubtedly one of the great tempests of the Atlantic. Only three men among the passengers were immune from sickness. James Galloway, John Henderson and my father. James when a young man had served onboard a man of war. Was onboard the *Windsor Castle* (a first rate seventy tons) going through the Dardinelles to Constantinople, with Admiral Duckworth's fleet. From a mortar cut in the solid rock on the bank the Turks threw a stone weig[h]ing eight hundred pounds. It went through the broadside of the *Windsor Castle*, broke her mainmast ricocheting on the deck killed several men. This stone was brought home to London and is one of the curios of Windsor Castle today. It was said to be French engineers that plan[n]ed and executed the feat, thought at the time to be a masterpiece of engineering.

John Henderson and my father had been [on] short voyages from Peterhead to Leith and other co[a]st towns. During the [xxx] storm these three men did all the cooking that was required which consisted chiefly in making water brose,[99] brochan[100] and **[31]** gruel. An old sailor, William

---

99. Brose is porridge made by boiling water and pouring it on oatmeal, then leaving it to stand for a short time with no further cooking.

100. Brochan is similar only with something added to the brose. This is a Gaelic word.

Gregory, who had many a day chased the huge fish about Baffin's old bay, and has sailed around the world by the Horn and Good Hope. Had been baptised a true son of Neptune when crossing the line, came down to put things in ship shape again that had been disarranged by the storm. Being interrogated by some of the women folk about the ship being lost during the great storm, and if it had not been the greatest tempest he had ever experienced. He hitched his trousers, turned his cud, smiled feebly and said signally, a little squally rather squally wind has veered a point or two fair weather bye and bye. Inured to storms this old <u>Jack Tar</u> regarded what the passengers thought a terrific hurricane as rather squally. He was considered the best steerer of the crew. As he walked aft to the poop to take his spell at the helm he would give a sly wink to any of the elder woman on deck which plainly said if you want a good sound sleep go to bed. His feet planted firmly on the deck, the spokes of the wheel grasped in his hand as in a vice, his souwester back from his forehead, his eyes on the sails and the sea in the ships course. He rolled from larboard to starboard and the brig glided over the huge waves like a sea bird.

The remainder of the voyage to the banks of Newfoundland was rather monotonous, seldom a fair wind for any len[g]th of time. When it did come, every inch of canvas was spread to <u>woo</u> the favoring gale. Whether custom or superstition I never heard discussed, but when in a dead calm, every male on board was ordered to whistle with all their might to make wind. Sailors would scan the ocean [32] for a cat's paw on the water. Often our ears would be greeted with blow breezy blow and I'll give you a <u>sugar</u>[?]. To whistle in a storm was an unpardonable offence. I think about ten knots an hour was our greatest speed even with a fair wind. Although a number of vessels were seen in mid-ocean, only two came close enough to speak. Since steam navigation has shortened the voyage across the Atlantic to an average of ten days, it may be that the fashion, the old custom of vessels speaking to each other is of rare occurrence, perhaps obsolete. Wireless telegraphy with the regular lines is likely practised. A ship bound for any American port from a British port, meets a vessel homeward bound, or comes within hailing distance in any case reports the other as so many days out all well as the case may be. This would be reported in British or American papers.

In our case both vessels were bound for America. The first one a brig bound for Boston from Newcastle with steam engines hardly as large as our own. When our Captain was speaking and nearly all our passengers and sailors looking on (the European that was her name), she appeared to suddenly stop or rather fall back, when we heard our sailors whispering to one another, "we've caught her wind. She's only an old coal tub. We'll show her down below before night." Whatever was the phenomenon was not explained, but by night her top mast was dimly visible away astern. The other ship was bound for Quebec, with passenger like ourselves, I have in sight above the horizon on our starboard, early in [**33**] the morning. Her main top gallant mast and [xxxxx] just above the horizon to windward, but by midday she was nearly up to us. A large ship a thousand tons burden or more the sailors said. She timed[101] way above our little brig which no doubt appeared li[l]liputian in contrast though hailing distance apart. There was a stiff gale and high sea running, but she forged ahead almost under bare poles. She altered her course to larboard with the intention of speaking. My father's Ward Helen Miller had a sharp tongue, and she was likewise mealy mouthed with the use of it. She had conceived a dislike to the Stuart family, and declared the big ship was a British frigate sent out to catch the *Alert* under suspicion of an absconding debtor being onboard. She appealed to the oldest sailor in the ship if she was not correct that action was often taken to recapture truant debtors that her port holes were now being opened ready to fire if the *Alert* did not heave too, immediately when the signal was given. Old William favoured her opinion. The Stuart family were in great tribulation ready to fawn at the feet of those they thought would render them protection. But the big ship came up without flying a signal or opening her portholes. She was now within hailing distance. We could distinguish people like ourselves waving towards us. We could almost see the outline of their features. In the meantime our Captain had got out his speaking trumpet and standing on the Poop put his mouth to the mouth of an enormous[102] brass thing like a bugle horn, and then rang across[103] the waves "What ship ahoy, dwelling on hoy." Then came back distinctly the *Clio* of Alloway. What's your cargo, passengers. We're[104] bound for [**34**] Quebec ahoy. Then followed the same formula from our ship. By night the *Clio* was sinking out of our sight away on her course towards Quebec. Such is the wonderful different in the speed of sailing vessels with the same wind and apparently equal[l]y laden according to size and cargo.

Occasionally the blow of a whale was seen seemingly a short distance from the ship, but the sailors said it was several miles away. For two days shoals of Porpoises as far as the eye could reach. On either side of the ship were swimming eastward at least the reverse of the ship's course. The Captain said they always swim against the wind, dorsal fin above water. A few dolphins one day swam around the ship, sailing at her best, and it did not seem to hurry them in the least.

Everyone enjoyed excellent health. The young people could eat and sleep to satisfy the most fastidious of health Savants. My chum Sandy Henderson and I were often bribed by the cook to bring him up a bucket of

---

101. He may have been trying to write "towered."

102. He wrote this with a -u- in front of the -r-.

103. He wrote this with two c's.

104. AB "where."

potatoes from the hold, with a cabin biscuit apiece, and cabin butter spread on them in non-stinted manner with his great big thumb.

The heaving of the lead to ascertain the ship's speed or rate of sailing I do not fully understand. A heavy lead attached to a line is thrown out, another line with knots on it at regular intervals. A knot is a nautical mile or geographical mile. It is one sixteen of a mean degree of a [meridian] on the earth's surface. I think it is longer by eight hundred feet than a statute mile. A sailor stands with a sand glass in his hand and just as soon as the first knot strikes the water he turns the lass, and the number of knots that run out [when] [35] the sand runs to the opposite end of the glass is the ship's speed an hour.

In very stormy days only a few of the men went up to do a little cooking. The galley was simply a box like thing perhaps 12 or 14 feet square, a door on each side opposite each other from larboard to starboard. On the forward side was a large grate intended for the passengers to cook on. On the opposite side was the ship's coppers, a curious arrangement, half store half furnace. It was divided into two compartments, the larger for soup, the smaller for boiling beef and pork. The sailors' meals were varied, during the week, especially their dinners. I could not tell the days the different dinners were served, but I remember some of the names as mentioned by the cook and cabin boy. There was barley broth, peas soup (split peas) with a great chunk of beef boiled in it, lapseuse, a seuse[105] which contained small pieces of beef about an inch square, boiled with potatoes all mashed together, perhaps some kind of seasoning in it. It was served like soup in kids. Small wooden vessels, not turned like a caup,[106] but like a most exquisite little tub. This only refers to their dinners, they had occasionally porridge for breakfast-called layue ate with treacle they had coffee, ,and I think tea but found by themselves. On Sundays they had duff, plum[107] pudding boiled in a bag. It might not have been compounded according [to] cookery book etiquette or hygiene science, but nevertheless relished judging from the manner it disappeared from the kids. They lived well so far as good substantial food was concerned.

There was no order observed among the passenger in regards to [36] the use of the fire, it was who can get their pot or pan on first. The cookhouse or galley was set first immediately in front of the long boat aft of the foremast. It must have been made of iron or it could not have withstood the intense heat that prevailed in it every day. A short funnel to each fire was contended to convey the smoke a short distance above the roof. But perhaps no mechanical contrivance[108] ever fell shorter of its intentions. Only

---

105. Both are types of porridge.

106. This is perhaps a Scots dialect spelling of "cup."

107. He spelled this with a –b-, perhaps one reason why the first two letters were underlined.

108. AB "conturveance."

about half a dozen persons could conveniently[109] stand inside of it. One of the doors had to be left open according to the wind. Often a sudden gust of wind would whirl the smoke about in all directions.

The ship's cook was a fine fellow. Always kind to the passengers, assisted them all in his power with their cooking. His very name indicated good nature; it was plain Peter Craig. The cabin boy Jamie Hogg nephew of mad Jamie was a little tyrant. He was known to the passengers by the diminutive Hoggie. When he found a few boys in the galley. It was out o' galley sheu out o' galley you d…d lubbers. There was a peculiar three legged stove in the galley. I suppose for the cook to rest when tired standing watching the cooking. One day Hoggie was imprimis[110] on this stool and Jessie G on his knee they occupied a large part of the passage, for Jamie had ample proportions especially in latitude. Jock Stuart was in the act of pouring boiling water from his tinpot into his caup of meal to make his brose. Un some untoward manner a collision between Jock, Hoggie and Jessie caused the contents of Jock's tinpot instead of going into the caup to make the [brine sueut] on to Hoggies feet. One of them was severely burned. When the stocking was withdrawn the skin came along with it. [37] By the young people Jock was severely blamed for the catastrophe. But the Matrons said Jessie was an idle hizzie an sud hae been burnt instead o' Hoggie. The best remedies available were administered to his feet. One of the elder women going down to the forecastle every day and dressing his feet until he could do so himself. It was two weeks before he appeared on deck again. If this was Hoggies initiation in courting it was not ominous of future success. But poor Hoggies days were of short duration. Three years after our voyage he came of age and his Uncle made him skipper of the *Alert*. On his first voyage to Quebec he arrived in due time, got the brig laden with timber, and left Quebec homeward bound in good order. But the *Alert* never returned. Inquiries were made at many seaports concerning the missing *Alert*, without gaining any information of a reliable character concerning her disappearance. The captain of some vessel reported that he saw in midocean a brig answering to the description of the *Alert*, a white band around her hull half way between the water line and deck, whirl around sever times and go down. The Peterhead people did not think this could be the *Alert*, as she was laden with timber and unlikely to go down in a calm day as reported. None of the crew that sailed with us were with the unfortunate Hoggie in his first and last voyage as Captain of the ill fated *Alert*. We heard from Peterhead that Hoggies crew were the riff raff of the town for his mate downwards. Good trusty seamen belonging to the town would not ship with so young and inexperienced a Captain.

In 1819 the first Steamship crossed the Atlantic. It was [38] simply an

---

109. He spelled it "conveniently."

110. Latin for "first." He wrote it as "imprimpis."

The Memoirs of Alexander Brodie

experiment. For several years there was no regular line of Steamers. I think the *Great Britain, Great Western* and *Sarah Sands*[111] were the first regular liners that carried the mails and passengers. They were side wheeled vessels and were toys in comparison to the Ocean Steamers of the present day. The screw or propeller coming into general use later on with the Cunard and Allan lines.

In 1835 and previous to that date, and several years later there was no such thing as Steamers carrying passengers to Quebec. The Allan had not yet matured their line. At the times referred to passengers had to find their own provision for a six to eight weeks voyage[112], and as I have told above cook as best they could with stinted convenience and often stinted supply of fresh water. There were[113] no assisted passages in those days. Everyone had to find his own fare. The paupers, Barnardo waifs, Duk[h[obors,[114] Gallicians,[115] nor foreign element to ally the blood of the true Briton.[116]

No doubt great improvements have taken place since 1835. Few ships then carried passengers as regular freight. The passengers' quarters were merely improvised for the time being, then knocked down and stowed away to make room for timber which was the general cargo home. For all I know there may be no such thing as a sail vessel carrying passengers from British ports to Quebec in 1906.

The ship's crew was divided into watches, starboard and larboard, the Captain having one, the mate the other, the order of the watches was changed by what was called the dog watch,[117] so that every watch had equal shares of day and night. The manner of calling the watch on the *Alert* was very simple. [39] When the time came a sailor took a han[d]spike used on the windless for raising the anchor, holding it erect he stru[ck] it vigour[ou]sly on deck several times close by the hatch then [clew ?] it and called in loud voice larboard, starboard watch ahoy. The watch below sprang from their hammocks dressed were on deck in a few minutes. The watch relieved were in their hammocks as soon as the others were on deck.

Before sighting Newfoundland we passed many fishing ships and schooners, also several large icebergs. Numberless pieces of ice floated

111. The *Great Western* was launched in 1838, the first Atlantic-crossing steamship, and for a few years the largest passenger ship in the world. The *Great Britain*, launched in 1843, was the longest ship in the world until 1854, and could cross the Atlantic in 14 days. The *Sarah Sands* was built in 1846.

112. They landed in Quebec on May 21, almost seven weeks after their departure from Peterhead on April 3.

113. AB "was."

114. See Back Stories in this chapter.

115. See Back Stories in this chapter.

116. See Back Stories in this chapter.

117. From 4 p.m. to 8 p.m.

close by the ship. The presence of ice so near seemed to lower the temperature several degrees. There appeared to be an awe parade both crew and passengers when passing icebergs. The mate stood on the bow with spyglass at his eye scanning the western horizon in case [t]he bergs should be in one course. Away on our larboard bow a large berg hove in sight. It passed about a mile distant, the Captain said, but is appeared be much nearer. Its top which was crested with snow appeared to be as high as the crosstrees of our main mast. The mate viewing it through the large spyglass said the side nearest to us was at least over a mile in length and the surfs dashed against its sides as on a rocky co[a]st relentlessly.

A few of the passengers were anxious to try their luck cod fishing, but the wind being form[id]able the captain refused to delay and give them a fair chance. He however furnished them with a line and bait. A heavy sinker was attached to the line and it ran out speedily. In about twenty minutes or half an hour two men drew it up, while others stood by on the lee side in expectation of seeing several large cod [40] on the hooks, but the bait came up as it went down to the great disappointment of the passengers who no doubt longed for a change of diet.

My remembrance of Newfoundland from the ship is of a cold desolate looking place. Whether we went through the Straits of Belle Isle, round by Cape Race to enter the Gulf of St. Lawrence I do not know, but I remember we looked at the land from the starboard side, which would indicate we were to the south of it. It may be we looked upon Cape Race, it being the southwestern extremity of the Island. A late writer says of the place, "It is the most important headland in the world. It has also a most unenviable notoriety. Its ill repute arises from the long and dreadful catalogue of shipwrecks. It is truly named the grave yard of the Atlantic."

We however saw the base and barren looking hills of Labrador. Some of the young people expressed a desire, a longing desire to get ashore and have a good run on them hills. The hills looked enticing enough for a run viewed from the ship. But intensely severe climate and utter desolation is the character given by explorers, and those who have lived as fishermen in this melancholy land.

When fairly within the Gulf the voyage became very interesting. A signal hoisted for a Pilot was not regarded for a few days although many small swift sailing craft passed[118] and repassed[119] at a distance. A feeling of disappointment appears, seemed to pervade all onboard because a pilot was not forthcoming. Hogg whose foot was not well again was sent aloft on the mainmast to scan the horizon for the sail of a pilot vessel. After rocking [41] back and forth from the larboard to starboard for a minute or two he called out, sail on the larboard bow. In a minute our signal for a

118. AB "past."
119. AB "repast."

pilot floated the mizzen peak. In [a] quarter of an hour a sail could be seen just above the horizon from the deck. The *Alert* altered her course towards the sail. It soon became evident the sail was bearing down towards us. In the afternoon the Sloop was alongside. The rope ladder was cast over the leeside and a little pleasant looking Frenchman clim[b]ed on deck. Shook hands with the Captain and mate (and of course was the cynosure of the passengers), his chest was hoisted onboard and carried to the cabin. He waved adieu to the men in the Sloop, and this little man became the Autocrat to all onboard until we arrived in Quebec.

A pilot in those days was a very important personage, and I suppose is so to this day. He had to know every bay, and headland, currents, tides and soundings in the Gulf and river. Hade to sail three voyages to Europe, pass a rigid examination, receive a diploma before he could act as a pilot. He was very intelligent of what he had seen and come under his personal observation, willing to give information to anyone in respect to his calling. He was very affable and suave in conversation, pleased to give information to anyone interested about places along the Gulf and river, notable in early [F]rench history. His home was a good way below Quebec, he pointed out his house on the river side, on the bank, hoisted a little flag and immediately another flag waved from a pole in front of the house. This was a signal to his family he had got a ship and was well. He said pilots had various avocations they followed during winter. He was a sailmaker and found ready sale in Quebec for all he could make during winter. Never heard how he was **[42]** Remunerated for his services.

A great many white whales,[120] or porpoises gamboled as if in play, sometimes leaping clear out of the water. Numbers of Solan[121] geese, and swans flew around often lighting near the ship. The cabin passenger fired a few shots at them but failed to get one. All the sailors had made several voyages to Quebec before, and knew the names of many places along the Gulf and river, Gaspe, Cape Chat, Point Outardes and many other places famous in early [F]rench settlements along the river.

Grosse Isle the quarantine Station is sel[d]om noticed by that name at least on the map. Said to be forty miles below Quebec. I do not think it was inhabited in 1835 only by government officials during winter only in the navigable season. During the years 1832 and 1833 the cholera had been very malignant. Many seamen and passengers died, few recovered when once smitten, hence every ship had to be thoroughly clean before going up to Quebec. No sooner was the *Alert* anchored than a small boat flying a yellow flag came alongside and Dr. Douglas[122] medical health officer clim[b]ed onboard. He arranged all passengers and seamen on file on

120. He was probably talking about belugas here.
121. These are now known as the Northern gannet.
122. See Back Stories in this chapter.

the deck. As his visit was anticipated a hurried dressing was performed to look as clean and well as circumstances would present. He was a tall strong looking Scotchman, grizzled whiskers and the lines on his face, sombre to appearance but indicated that what he said he meant. He scrutinized every one with [A]rgus[123] eyes, even our baby did not escape his inspection. He ordered all passengers ashore, likewise all bedding and wearing apparel not in use. In short all things of cloth kind for inspection and the breaths to be whitewashed. The sailors apartment[124] underwent a baptism also. It is a mystery [43] where dust comes from aboard a ship at sea.

The longboat was hoisted out from amidships and lowered alongside, passengers went first, then luggage, could not say how many trips back and forth from the ship until all was ashore. The boat was run in on a shingly beach not many feet about the level of the river. The chests and boxes of different shapes and sizes were carried from the boat and arranged on the beach, lids unlocked or knocked off everything topsy turvie. Women folk in sad perplexity but looking out for their own things. Human nature can err under such circumstances as well as anywhere else.

The co[a]st appeared to be precipitous and rocky down the river from the landing place. Near to the landing just above high tide mark a man had a small shed, a kind of counter in front. He was doing a flourishing business selling prunes and spruce beer, but before returning to the ship there was ample evidence that John Barley corn in a more concentrated state was at least Cousin German to the spruce beer.

My chum and I had a good run over the rocks. We started away to what seems to me (now) to have been woods, but were stopped by a sentinel there. I presume to keep order and prevent mutinous conduct among seamen. He did not seem to be under very strict di[s]cipline for he found an old chum in Sandy Morrison. He was a [B]uchan laddie and Sandy and him had a good crack on youthful pleasures years ago where herd laddies although on duty.

Back Stories of Chapter Four

The *Alert*

In 1981, when I visited Peterhead, I went down to the harbour. I wanted to see the ocean more or less as how the Brodies had seen in it 1835. What caught my eye, though, was not the ocean, but a tugboat that bore the name *Alert*. I greeted it as one descendant of the trip to another.

The *Alert* of Peterhead was a 192-ton brig. Brigs were a relatively small type of ship used to carry passengers across the Atlantic. The term "brig"

---

123. Argus is a Latinized form of the Greek mythical character Argo, who was a giant with 100 eyes.

124. He wrote this word with two p's.

comes from "brigantine," which ultimately came from "brigand" as pirates often used this size and type of ship. Brigs had two masts, both of which were square-rigged. In Lucille H. Campey's book on historic Aberdeen sailing ships that carried passengers, there is a table of ships that carried 60 or more Scottish emigrants to "British America" from 1801 to 1855. The brigs had a tonnage range of 141 to 312, barques (which had three masts) 250 to 510 tons, and ships to 709 tons (Campey 202: 95–8). Most of the boats listed were larger than the *Alert*.

The *Alert* was first used as a whaling vessel hunting off of the shores of Greenland, beginning in 1817, when its whalers had killed eight whales (Buchan 1819: 23). At the time of the Brodie voyage, James Hogg was the owner, not the captain. In 1835, she sailed under Captain W. Boyd. That year she left Peterhead on April 3 and arrived on May 21 in Quebec. There was one cabin passenger; everyone else, including the Brodies, was in steerage. The new rules (as of 1835) governing how many passengers ships were allowed to carry set a maximum of three passengers per five tons ship weight, so she would be allowed a little over 100 passengers. The ship took another trip that year, again with Captain Boyd, leaving sometime early in July and arriving on August 27 (www.theshipslist.com/ships/Arrivals/1835.a/shtml; and Dobson, David and Kit Dobson [2009], *Ships from Scotland to North America, 1830–1860*, vol. 2, Baltimore: Clearfield Company, page 6).

It is hard to track the *Alert*'s subsequent fate as there were a number of ships with that same name. There was even one that sailed out of Aberdeen. The most famous one was built in Boston in 1828, and was featured in the diary and novel of American writer Richard Henry Dana in his best-seller *Two Years Before the Mast: A Personal Narrative of Life at Sea*, first published in 1840, in which he describes his two-year trip beginning in 1834 from Boston, around the southern tip of South America to California.

James Hogg

A "Hogg. J." from Peterhead was listed as captaining the *Invincible* as a whaler in 1819, 1821 and 1823 (www.explorenother.com/whalers/features/whalecaptains1.htm). A James Hogg of Peterhead survived the wrecking of three ships in the Davis Strait area: the *Invincible* in 1822, the *Enterprise* in 1828, and the *James* in 1831. In 1834 a Captain Hogg was the master of the Alert (Dobson 2009: 6). In 1836, he captained the *Resolution*. He would die by drowning, however, when the sea wall that protected the Peterhead harbour was destroyed by a storm in 1849. He was 55 at the time. His body was never recovered (Sutherland 1993: 18, 21 and 31).

John Steckley
The Later Immigrants
The **Doukhobors** are a Russian religious sect, dissenters from the Orthodox church, who encouraged a radical pacificism which entailed not fighting in the Russian army. They were fiercely persecuted by the tsars from the time of their 18th-century origins. In 1899, 7,500 came to Canada (mostly Saskatchewan), and in 1902 500 more.

Galician is a term used at the time to refer to Ukrainians who came to Canada bringing the same dreams and with the same government encouragement as did the Brodies. From 1891 to 1914 possibly as many as 200,000 Ukrainians came to Canada (primarily the Prairies) as farmers for the great expanses of land that had formerly belonged to Aboriginal people. Most Ukrainians were officially designated as "the enemy" in World War I, as a good part of the Ukraine was controlled by the Austro-Hungarian Empire. This resulted in Ukrainian concentration camps spread across Canada during the war. See *First Wave of Ukrainian Immigrants to Canada, 1891–1911*, www.virtualmuseum.ca/sgc-cms/histoires_de_chez_nous-community-memories/pm_v2.php?id=story_line&lg=English.

The **"Barnardo waifs"** were British orphans or children of the poor who from 1882 to 1939 were sent to Canada to live with farm families by Thomas Barnardo, an Irish man who ran an organization to take care of such children. The ones coming to Canada had to be at least 14 years old. These people were "true Britons" too. See Bagnell, Kenneth (2001), *The Little Immigrants: The Orphans Who Came to Canada* (Toronto: Dundurn).

Dr. George Douglas
Dr. George Douglas (1809–1864), was born in Carlisle, Scotland, and would distinguish himself in Canadian medical history by his work with the Irish victims of the potato famine (actually a fungus that killed only potatoes), in 1847. After leaving Scotland, he went to the U.S. in 1822, became a licensed doctor in 1827, and was the medical superintendent at the Gaspé quarantine station in 1832, assisting at Grosse Isle until 1836 when he became the medical superintendent there.

Sicknesses and Deaths on Grosse Isle
From Thomas Strathroy (1849), "Emigrant Sickness of 1847," *The Edinburgh Medical and Surgical Journal* 72: 95 (Edinburgh: Andrew and Charles Black):

Year	Number of Emigrants	Admitted to Hospital	% Admitted to Hospital	Deaths	% Deaths
1835	11,580	126	1.08%	10	7.93%
1847	98,106	8,691	8.86%	3,288	37.36%

Cholera in 1832

Before it came to Canada, cholera had moved across continental Europe to Britain. In 1832, it came across the Atlantic to Quebec by means of the thousands of immigrants coming from Britain that year. It struck a Lower Canada divided politically and without a sound health care system in place, and about 8,000 people died, most of them British immigrants. This had a profound effect on the city of Quebec, which had a population of some 20,000, and Montreal, with a population of roughly 30,000 at the time. One of the first moves was to establish Gross Isle, a small island (7.7 square kilometres) some 30 miles downriver from Quebec, as a quarantine station.

The key to stopping cholera was in improving how human wastes were dealt with, as the disease spread through the water, not directly from contact with the infected. As there were no sewers and regular waste removal at the time in Quebec and Montreal, the disease could spread fast. Overcrowded Atlantic-crossing ships made good breeding grounds for the bacteria *Vibrio cholera* (which wasn't identified as the cause until decades later), which produced a toxin in the small intestine that made the stomach more porous to water, with predictable results. The best protected places were local forts, as orders to clean up the handling of water were taken seriously there.

Cholera struck Canada again in 1834, 1849, 1851, 1852 and 1854.

Chapter Five
Crossing the Atlantic and Arriving in Grosse Isle

A long open shed stood back conspicuously from the [**44**] beach perhaps a hundred yards. On the back wall, on the inside, was painted in large black letters, English, Scotch, Irish. So far as I can remember there was no partition between the different apartments.[125] A particular friend of ours who came to Canada in 1834 wrote on the back of the shed with a piece of chalk, this graphic description of it in rhyme.

> All you that happens to come here[126]
> Take care and keep you clean
> Or else they will detain you
> When you come to quarantine
> The[y]'l spread you out upon a rock
> That is both rough and bare
> And cram you in an open shed
> Tho' you should perish there.

I think the sheds were only used when a ship had to ride quarantine until her passengers were reported clean by the health officer. A large gaudy looking brig, with Pomona of Dublin in large bright colours on her stern and crosstrees, lay at anchor a short distance down the river from our ship. She had been detained a week waiting until her passengers were duly purified. Garments of many hues and shapes were spread on the rocks drying and being gathered up to be conveyed on board again. There I at least got my first sight of Paddy from Cork, not with his coat buttoned Behind according to the old adage,[127] for as near as my chum and I could judge there were[128] few buttons to button either in front or behind. The men all wore knee breeches, and low shoes. Some had long-waisted, long

---

125. AB "appartments."

126. I have not found reference to these lines anywhere. This might just be the only remaining written recording of these dire words of warning.

127. This was part of a 19th century stereotype of the presumed foolishness of an Irish man. Uncle Alex was probably thinking at the time of the then popular song *The Bold Irishman*, about a man from Cork who goes to London. In the fourth stanza we have the following:

> A blustering bully with a head like a Turk
> Says welcome from Ireland, sweet Paddy from Cork
> Arrah turn you around Pat, for I've been a kin
> For I never yet see a coat buttoned behind.
> (http://sites.google.com/a/umn.edu/mh/home/Irishman-html)

128. AB "was."

tailed coats. Could not say whether this style of coat had any affinity to the now almost obsolete swallow [45] tail or the swallow to the Irish patron. The women looked tidy enough to appearance, some very short skirts and han[d]kerchiefs around their heads. My chum and I went as near as heard them conversing in an unknown tongue to us. They spoke fast as if actuated by some impulse. From subsequent knowledge of Irish nationality, I think these people must have come from the extreme south, or west of Ireland. I question whether there exists, now, after the lapse of nearly three quarters of a century, such sons and daughters in the green Isle as the passengers of the Pomona.

On board the *Alert* again waiting for the incoming tide to move up to Quebec. In the morning saw the falls of Montmorency, Wolf[e]'s Cove, the [P]lains of Abraham, the tin roofs and Steeples of upper Quebec glistening in the morning sun. Coming nearer, cannon frowned from the ramparts and citadel of the Gibraltar of the [N]ew [W]orld.

A forest of masts dark[e]ned the vision as we looked up the great river. The anchor dropped and as if by some majestic wand had been waved over the ship. Her sails were close reefed and the *Alert* swung round to the ebb tide. I was very much astonished next morning to find Quebec on the opposite side of the river. Even the explanation that the tide had turned failed to reconcile me. The Captain went ashore in his gig, or rather what he called the stern boat, about some business about disembarking. He came back in a short time, and said that all who were aim[ing to][129] leave the ship, could do so tomorrow[130] as the *St. George* a large Montreal Steamer would sail in the morning.

Being the last time we would all be together again on this [46] side of eternity. A kind of festal gathering or thanksgiving was held in the half deck. Captain, Mate, Cabin passenger and a few of the sailors not on duty were guests. The board was spread with all the dainties improvised of course for the occasion, which was enough, but perhaps might scarcely[131] grace a similar occasion in 1906. Thanks given by James Galloway the dainties partaken of. Then followed songs, and responses very flattering to Captain, crew and ship, and if it was in their power to give advice to those coming to America from Peterhead to come in the *Alert*, and no storms nor ice need fear. After drinking success to Captain Boyd[132] and his Jolly crew the meeting ended with well wishes to all.

The meeting though ostensibly a farewell, yet to the fathers and moth-

---

129. I am not sure of what is written here as it is at the extreme end of the paper, often a difficult place to read from in the manuscript, and it looks to me like he simply wrote "aimed" before "leave."

130. AB "tommorow."

131. AB "scracely."

132. AB "Boid."

ers, it was a time for inward rejoicing. Their minds were bent on what they braved the perils of six weeks on the billows of the wide Atlantic to accomplish. To materialize a new home, a more independent life for themselves and children, they had left their homes, perhaps humble homes, nevertheless dear homes to every true son and daughter of the land that gave us birth, whose every square foot is Classic. They had left the society of many dear friends and relations. They had come to a land and with few exceptions a strange people. The future was void wholly yet in fancy. The old homes across the sea would often be visited in dreams of the night and reveries of day. Pleasant memories of the past. Sunny memories to the weary who "ne'er return to their ain countree". Although a digression, I cannot refrain from quoting a few lines[133] from the *Scottish Exile's [F]arewell*:

The Scottish Exile's Farewell – Thomas Pringle
We seek a wild and distant shore   [47]
Beyond the Atlantic main
We leave thee to return no more
Or view thy cliffs[134] again
But may dishonor blight our fame
And quench our household fires
When we or ours forget thy name
Green Island of our Sires
Our native land our native vale
A long and last [a]dieu
Farewell to bonny Teviotdale[135]
And Scotland's mountains blue

The leaving of the old *Alert* was the realizing of a long anticipated event, not that the voyage had been disagreeable or unsocial as voyages go, but the desired object of the passengers was ever before their mental vision to get that new home away still in fancy though arrived in Canada.

It would perhaps be unique for young men and young women having free access to each other's company for six weeks and be immune from the influence of the little blind god. There were[136] at least t[w]o young men, and two young girls [who] had no desire to bid farewell to the old *Alert*. They would have preferred if possible if the voyage would have continued

---

133. These lines are a little different from those of the actual poem. See Back Stories in this chapter.

134. AB "clifts."

135. Teviotdale is an old name for the area of the southeast border of Scotland now known as Roxburghshire. It is where the poet Thomas Pringle, who wrote this poem, came from. See Back Stories in this chapter.

136. AB "was."

Ad infinitum.[137] One young lady was so severely wounded by Cupid's dart for a young sailor that she went home again with the first opportunity from Quebec and ultimately married the young Jack Tar. The other young man after swearing undying love to his girl, and God as witness to the contract, and she solemnly accented to the agreement she would [48] wed no other man but he. Well he was employed by an agent of the Hudson's Bay Company in Montreal. Went away to the far North Regions and married a half bre[e]d Squaw. The girl who was to be so faithful in love, like Imogene of old,[138] soon forgot her vows for another fellow had "caught her affections so light and so vain and carried her home as his spouse."[139] There was no need for a ghost coming back to recriminate. It was a Bona Fide case of natural dissolution. I have heard gossips aver that Geordie nor Annie would not remove the face cloth and take a peep at their dead love.[140] Broken vows are hard to mend, and in many cases are better unmended.

Small boats propelled by side wheels or paddles driven on the same principle as the old horse power threshing machines the horses walking around on deck, plied from ship to wharf taking off passengers and luggage.

The Stuarts and Galloways determined to remain a short time in Quebec. Our family and the Hendersons (of whom my Chum was a member) and the rest of the passengers were anxious to leave the ship and proceed up country as fast as possible. We were put ashore on an old rickety wharf, but just how our luggage was transferred to the *St. George* at another wharf I have no recollection.

We however got on board her in the evening. She was the largest boat on the river from Quebec to Toronto in 1835 except the *John Bull*.[141] Of course these two boats could go no further than Montreal. My chum and I ran up a narrow street a short distance from the wharf. An old woman sat close to the wall with a small stand, with a few sweeties and gingerbread. Chum pointed to a cake of gingerbread asked the price of it. She said un sou. [49] We knew nothing of but we held out to her a French money a bawbee apiece. A bawbee in Scotland is the common name of half penny. She grab[b]ed the bawbees with eagerness [and] smile[d] pleasantly as if she had done a good stroke of business. We subsequently learned we had

---

137. AB "infinetum." A Latin phrase meaning "forevermore."

138. Imogene (usually spelled Imogen) was a legendary Celtic queen, and appeared as a princess in Shakespeare's play *Cymbeline*.

139. This is from the poem written by Matthew Gregory Lewis (1775–1818), *Alonzo the Brave and the Fair Imogine*.

140. He is referring here to Geordie Scott and Annie Graeme in Scottish writer James Hogg's (1770–1835) epic poem *Geordie Scott: A Hamely Pastoral*.

141. The *John Bull*, launched in 1831, could generate 260 horsepower (Mackey 2000: 80). It did not last long, as it was destroyed by fire in 1839, killing some 40 people.

paid her twice what she had asked for her gingerbread. As we turned away to run back to the boat she said something away beyond our linguistic knowledge. She bid us good bye in her native language. <u>Au revoir</u>, or [c]a va or …

It was quite dark when the *St. George* left the wharf for Montreal. She had a crowd of passengers, Scotch, English, Irish and a great number of French Canadians, raftsmen returning to Bytown[142] (Ottawa), to bring down more rafts. Down below in the passenger quarters on each side, were berths one above another from the cabin to the bow. I do not think there was any bedding in them. As far as I remember my father lifting me into an upper berth just at that precise moment. I observed a Negro crawling in a berth a little further on. This was my first sight of one of the seed of Ham.[143] I was somewhat apprehensive of going to sleep in a place where there was one of the race that killed Mungo Park.[144] Had heard Park's travels in Africa read by my father and mother in winter evenings, and commented on nowise complimentary to the Negro race, but my father assured me there was no danger to be apprehended.

Back Stories of Chapter Five

Pomona

Left Dublin on April 12 carrying with it 140 settlers, and arrived in Quebec on May 21. Left Dublin on August 1 and arrived on September 17—both trips with Stevens as the captain (www.theshipslist.com/ships/Arrivals/1835.a/shtml).

John Bull

Carried 32 cabin passengers and 177 in steerage for 209 total on July 2, 1835 arrival in Montreal (www.theshipslist.com/ships/passengerlists/1835/jbjuly02.shtml).

Thomas Pringle

Thomas Pringle (1789-1834), the poet who wrote *The Scottish Exile's Farewell*, was born in southeast Scotland, but emigrated to South Africa as part of a scheme to setttle the area with white people. He was physically disabled but was a skilled writer, so he did not engage in farming, but wrote

---

142. AB "Byetown," here as elsewhere.

143. Ham was one of the sons of Noah. Noah damned him for some grave sin that has never been made clear. The original interpretation was that this meant cursing Ham's son Canaan to servitude. Later, racist elements in the Christian, Jewish and Muslim faiths said that the curse caused the black skin of Africans, a result of the sin of their progenitor.

144. See Back Stories in this chapter.

of his new country in various newpapers that he was involved with. As he was strongly anti-slavery and poor, he was forced to leave South Africa to return to Britain. He did not go back to his homeland, but settled in London, where he dedicated his life to the anti-slavery movement. Slavery was abolished in Britain in 1833, the year before Pringle died.

The Scottish Exile's Farewell

Our native Land— our native Vale—
A long and last adieu!
Farewell to bonny Lynden-dale,
And Cheviot-mountains blue!

Farewell, ye hills of glorious deeds,
And streams renowned in song!
Farewell, ye blithesome braes and meads
Our hearts have loved so long!
Farewell, ye broomy elfin knowes,
Where thyme and harebells grow!
Farewell, ye hoary haunted howes,
O'erhung with birk and sloe!

The battle-mound, the Border-tower,
That Scotia's annals tell;
The martyr's grave, the lover's bower—
To each— to all— farewell!

Home of our hearts! our fathers' home!
Land of the brave and free!
The sail is flashing through the foam
That bears us far from thee.

We seek a wild and distant shore,
Beyond the Atlantic main;
We leave thee to return no more,
Nor view thy cliffs again.

But may dishonour blight our fame,
And quench our household fires,
When we, or ours, forget thy name,
 Green Island of our Sires!

Our native Land— our native Vale—
A long, a last adieu!

Farewell to bonny Lynden-dale,
And Scotland's mountains blue!

Mungo Park

Mungo Park (1771–1806) was the son of a well-to-do family who became first a doctor then an explorer in the interior of Africa. His written works and public presentations were influential in making people in Britain aware of Africa. On his last expedition he drowned in a river in Nigeria while fleeing local people who were attacking the intruder's boat. Many of them died shot to death by Park and his company. It is likely that what Uncle Alex's father read to him was the newly-published *Life of Mungo Park*, published by an anonymous H.B. in Edinburgh in 1835.

Chapter Six
Two Boats to the Interior

Taking the *St. George* from Quebec to Montreal

Next day Sabbath all our party up on the upper deck and as far as possible dressed in Sabbath day attire endeavouring [50] to reverence the Lord's day as best we could under present circumstances. But there was little sanctity for the Lord's day on board the *St. George* was soon manifest. As she made her way up the great river it widened out in many places almost to a lake. Lake St. Peter fifty or sixty miles below Montreal a good sized lake. The landscape was continually changing often very picturesque viewed from the steamer. Every few miles great rafts floated past on their way to Quebec. The French raftsmen assembled on the front part of the boat, on the upper deck, and danced with wonderful agility and vigour to the <u>deedle, eddle, lal dee laddle</u> of a little wizened[145] faced man with a red sash round his waist. The Scotch passengers looked on this scene with grave faces. My mother turned away with this remark, "We'er far frae hame."

The *St. George* called at many little places, towns or village to take on and let off passengers also freight of different kinds. No sooner was the boat alongside the wharf than a number of men, women, boys and girls were aboard selling bread, milk, apples, and small cakes of maple sugar. The sugar was the cynosure above everything else to the Scotch juveniles. Even some who were of advanced years were very enthusiastic on the good things in store for them in the land of promise. They longed for the opportunity to bore a hole in the almost sacred tree, and enjoy a feast of sweets without restraint.

The Negro was an important point of attraction to the Scotch children, and he used all his powers of pleasing to get a few little girls to come close up to him and take a bribe of maple sugar. He persevered until he got two to sit on his knee and [51] and seemed gratified at his success.

It was late on Sunday night when the *St. George* arrived at Montreal. Have no recollection whatever of the disembarkation. Only remember I awakened in what appeared to be an upper story of a large ware house near the river, by a very annoying and discordant noise. This noise had awakened the rest of the sleepers as well as myself. Heard mumbling and grumbling wakened so soon by that infernal noise. What on all the Earth could be making that worst of all noises ever heard before? When we got up and down from the upper story we soon ascertained it was the piping of frogs. I had seen many frogs and toads in Scotland. In Buchan we called frogs <u>poddicks</u>, but never heard of them making such a disagreeable noise as disturb sleep. We had an overplus of this kind of Orchestra before we

---

145. AB "wizzened."

reached Toronto.[146]

We remained in Montreal two or three days. Did not roam very far from our meantime habitation. There were[147] excellent piers and large vessels lying at them. This was many years before the advent of the Allan Steamer.[148] I have a dim remembrance of hearing these large vessels traded to the West Indies, brought sugar, molasses, rum and perhaps some tropical fruit.

We were astonished at the furious driving through the streets of Montreal. In Peterhead we never saw a horse off walk except in a coach, a gig or chaise or riding horse-back. The few days we were in Montreal were excessively warm, and with our sea going garments and scotch bonnets were much oppressed indeed. In a sort of back yard a little way from our abode a young girl was washing. Betty made a short acquaintance with her, and found a kindred spirit. She was an English girl, had been in Montreal [52] two years. She gave Betty valuable advice, told her to slip off her extra petticoats and stays as quick as possible at it was much warmer in Upper Canada than here.

Riding the *Mary Anne of Prescott*: A Durham Boat

In 1835 there were two forwarding companies in Montreal. One by barge up the Ottawa[149] to Bytown[150] thence by canal to Kingston.[151] The other by Durham boat through the Lachine canal and up the St. Lawrence to Kingston. Our party chose the St. Lawrence rout[e] for what reason I never heard.

Our Durham boat was a large stout build vessel. Her length of keel and breadth of beam I cannot tell. Suffice to say she was a superb vessel of her kind. There was not pretentious to elegance or scenic display about her. To give and receive hard knocks seemed to be the desideratum in construction, and intention. She also had the maidenly name of the *Mary Ann of Prescott*. She was equipped a good deal on the Lugger style. She had a mast and great square sail, long sweeping oars which like the mast and sail were only twice perhaps only [used] once during the voyage. She was drawn by horses sometimes by oxen, along the canal, and river bank. The French

---

146. Scottish frogs go by the scientific name of *Rana temporaria*, and utter a "soft, repetitive croak" (www.froglife.org/amphibians-and-reptiles/common-frog-2/). The same cannot be said for the bullfrogs or *Litobates catesbeianus* that are the much louder and weightier frogs that Uncle Alex would encounter near Montreal.

147. AB "was."

148. The Allan Shipping line was formed by Scottish Captain Alexander Allan in 1819. His son, Hugh Allan launched the Montreal Ocean Steamship Line in 1854.

149. AB "Ottaway."

150. Bytown became Ottawa in 1854.

151. AB "Kingstone."

boys driving the teams wore a kind of satchel slung over one shoulder in which was carried a small axe, whereby in case the current overcame the team the cable was hacked in two, and let the boat and all she contained go to Davie Joneses Locker. But the principal mode of propulsion was shoving her along with long poles, cleats were nailed along the deck on each side for foot holds. A man on each side stuck their poles in at the bow, simultaneously putting their shoulders to the head of the poles shove as they walked to the stern. When these got so far other two started and <u>Vic[e] versa</u>. When the mast was not in use it was laid from cabin to for[e]castle, (for she had both [53] places in a kind of way) it was raised about three of our feet above the deck. On it was stretched a tarpaulin[152] underneath was our home for nearly two weeks. Even this circumscribed abode was stuffed in every corner with great bales of goods leaving little room for the passengers' luggage. The tarpaulin was all the shelter we had from the sun and storms. The *Mary Ann* had been laid up for the night in a kind of cove. One of the shoring poles was stuck in the beach (in the mud) and to this pole she was moored for the night. The day had been very sultry and lonery [?] presaging a storm. The storm came during the night in great force. No doubt one of the great electric storms frequent in midsummer in Canada. The lightning[153] flashes ath[w]art the wide river and for an instant now and again showed our perilous condition. Rain had collected in the slack places of the tarpaulin, while the wind threw it into convolutions, down came the rain. The result a thorough baptism, but made unwelcome under the present circumstances. The *Mary Ann* rocked uneasily, for the cove which was placid and smooth as a mirror in the evening, was violently[154] agit[at]ed by the storm. She would run up the length of her cable, then back and careen from one side to the other. Whether the boatmen and passengers realized the danger we were in during the night, I never heard, but in the morning all looked abashed and seemed impressed with the fact that it was a Providential escape from a watery grave in the St. Lawrence. In the morning our danger was plain to be seen. The pole by being pulled from one side to the other by the movement of the boat was so loose that a child could have pulled it out. [54]

There was no bulwark or gunwale to protect children from going overboard. When I think of it after the lapse of seventy one years, it seems marvellous that some tragedy did not occur. One day our little sister was standing near the side of the boat when a large dog belonging to one of the passengers came running past, gave her a jostle to the outside of the boat. She lost her balance and fell over the side. She held on to the edge of the deck. I happened to be close by and caught her hands and called for help.

152. AB "tarpauline." Here and elsewhere.
153. AB "lightening."
154. AB "voilently."

John Steckley
Young Alex Gets Lost
If there was cause for anxiety on the minds of parents for their children crossing the Atlantic, it was a hundred times augmented in the Durham boat. Passengers were allowed to go off and walk along the river side. They had to do this in order to buy provisions for the biscuits and butter from Peterhead were nearly exhausted. There was no means of cooking on the *Mary Anne* at least for passengers. It was easy to beat her sailing along the river without much effort. She would not venture out in the river further than the poles could reach the bottom, consequently she had to keep in shore in every bend or cove making the passage much longer. Boys would get off and occasionally stray away too far inland from the river, not knowing whether they were ahead or behind the boat. One day I went off with four boys older than myself. The public road was some distance from the river, with apparently small farms between it and the river. We were in no hurry, observing whatever appeared strange to us or attracted our curiosity. We expected to meet the boat ay any time by going down to the river. We crossed (what I think now) was the Beauharnois Canal (just being excavated) on a narrow arched wooden bridge. Along the excavation on both sides were innumerable shanties as far as we could see. [55]

After leaving the canal we found a foot path leading down to the river through a ravine. The big boys thought we must be ahead of the boat and started back close to the edge of the river. I kept up to them until we came to a place where trees (probably willows) grew partly into the river, the branches extending quite a distance over the water. The big boys passed around holding by the branches. I tried to do the same, but the current was swift and strong, lifted me off my feet and I had still further to go out to get past. I turned back, and attempted to go through an orchard, at least I now suppose it was an orchard. Two men were working (perhaps planting or hoeing corn). They called loudly to me in a angry threatening manner. I thought they were going to arrest me for trespassing on their premises. I knew the danger there was in trespassing on people's enclosures around Peterhead. Most likely the men were telling me how I could get clear of my difficulties. I however ran back to the path we came down to the river, thinking to find the road we came when we left the boat in the morning. I could not find it. I was in great distress of mind, thought I was lost and would never see my father nor mother or the rest of the family again. In this dilemma my father found me. The big boys when they found the boat reported my condition hence my father found me by their direction.

The *Mary Ann* lingered along slowly, sometimes lay up for a day or two. The men said they were waiting for supplies. The passengers became very uneasy at the delay [and] threatened to prosecute the company. The boatmen only laughed. At last patience became unendurable and one of the passengers started away back to Montreal [56] to see if anything could be done to make them abide by the agreement. He had only gone about an hour when a wagon[155] came down the hill, the bank to the river with the much talked of supplies which consisted of a sheet iron stove. A very primitive[156] specimen of cooking stove, so much improved since the summer of 1835 that if the sheet iron convenience of the *Mary Ann* was placed side by side of the steel range of today, the evolution could scarcely be discerned. A few bags of potatoes, some ropes, two new men one of them to be the Captain. A young man started after the man who had gone on his way to Montreal and overtook him after a hard race.

Back Stories of Chapter Six

Beauharnois Canal

The original Beauharnois Canal measured 15 miles (24 km) in length and was built on the south side of the St. Lawrence River, opening in 1843. The canal became obsolete and was superseded in 1899 by the Soulanges Canal, which ran on the north side of the St. Lawrence River. The present Beauharnois Canal was built between 1929 and 1932 on the south side of the St. Lawrence River, measuring 24.5 km in length. This canal was built as part of a hydroelectric development at Beauharnois which saw a dam and power house built to take advantage of the drop of 24 m (83 feet) between Lake St. Francis and Lake St. Louis. Some of the electricity is used to power a large aluminum smelter.

In the 1950s, the Beauharnois Canal had two locks added as part of the St. Lawrence Seaway project. This in turn superseded the Soulanges Canal.

---

155. AB "waggon" here and elsewhere. From my reading of 19th century writers such as Catharine Parr Traill in her *The Backwoods of Canada*, I have learned that spelling "wagon" in this way was not unusual at that time.

156. AB "primitive."

Chapter Seven
The Trip Continues to Toronto

The Captain to be, a tall lanky rough looking man in exterior when not riled, quite affable, and full of anecdote[s] concerning life on the river. He would point out mounds on the banks of the river as the boat moved along slowly, the last resting places of victims of the terrible cholera morbus.[157]

In 1835 Steam boats did not run down the St. Lawrence from Kingston to Montreal as they do now. The canal system to escape the Long Sault rapids coming up was scarcely a matter of conjecture. The route by Bytown and Rideau Canal was to obviate the dangerous Sault rapids. Still there must have been parts of the river navigable for small steamers. I think it was Coteau de Lac. Some place however where there was a good wharf and passengers coming off a boat. The celebrated Bishop Macdonnell was pointed out to us as he walked up the wharf. A silver crucifix perhaps eight or ten inches in length on his ample breast. He was a renowned Minister of the church of Rome in Lower Canada in his day. He was greatly revered not only by his own church people, but by all denominations. [57] His contour indicated a man of great strength and vigour, mental and physical.

My memory is confused about many places along the river. Looking at the map does not agree with my impressions on my memory. Remember Lachine, Cedar Rapids, Coteau de Lac, Three Rivers,[158] but cannot place them in correct order. Supposing I were to come up the river at the present time, men, boats, and places would all be changed. The Durham boats have all gone from the St. Lawrence many years ago. Captain Tottershaw and his boatmen have exit[ed] from this scene never to return again. No crew of the same type of men, will sail a *Mary Ann* like ours from Montreal to Prescott as long as the St. Lawrence rolls its course to the sea. If any one of the crew be alive today, he must be a few years over the century mark and could tell many interesting reminiscences of danger and tragedies[159] on the river traf[f]ic. I have no thought however that one of them could be alive, they had the appearance of being mid aged men in 1835, and owing to the rough hazardous life their chances for long life were small.

Just what part of the river, and the name of the place, I have no distinct remembrance. It was quite wide and the current strong. It was crossing the river at this place that the mast sail oars were utilized.

It was quite a job raising the mast, hoisting the sail and getting the

---

157. The word "morbus" refers to diseases.

158. The first three follow the order in which they present them. I don't know what Three Rivers he is referring to, as the city of Trois Rivieres is down river from Montreal. There was probably some site up river of the other three that had that name at that time.

159. AB "tradegies."

oars at work for simply crossing the river. The boat notwithstanding all efforts, with sail and oars to keep her prow upstream lost way. Although a considerable distance between the Sault the current was not near so strong as on the Canadian side. In looking across the American side great rocks appeared [58] to be standing up out of the water, which was dashed into froth from one great boulder to another.

The sail was lowered, the mast placed amid ship again—as a sailor would say. A push then up river with the long poles. The men shoved with all their might the clear water swished into foam around the prow of the *Mary Ann*, and the Captain splashed at her stern with his long splasher[160] with wonderful dexterity. Next day all got off that could walk. The banks were high and steep occasionally it was necessary to go round a cove or bend in the river which brought us into brief acquaintance with rural life in northeastern [New] York State. Here I saw the first ear of Indian Corn, here I received the first sting of a bumble bee (on my cheek) in America when I had almost succeeded in harrying his bike.[161]

Riding a Durham Boat from Long Sault to Prescott

The following day the great event of the Durham boat experience was to be consummated. The ascent of the Long Sault. In the morning men, horses and oxen should have been on hand to pull the boat up through this dangerous current. They were not on time. The Captain swore all the oaths in his vocabulary, at the Yankees for not being on hand. He splashed as if he was annihilating all the Yankees in creation with his long sweeping thing at the stern. What he really did towards guiding or propelling the boat with this curious thing I have not the least idea. After he had exhausted all his known oaths, and got his breath an instant or two he invented new ones. He cursed every sense and member of their bodies.[162] He terrified the women folk, they could[163] hold their tongues no longer, and told him if he did not cease his blasphemy God's wrath would certainly fall on him and all onboard. What might have been the consequence of [59] this state of things continued much longer is unknown to finite mind, for just at that moment men, horses, and oxen were seen coming down the bank. The change in the Captain's demeanour[164] was quick as an electric shock. Whether he believed that his anathemas[165] had been carried to the Yankees

---

160. A "splasher" might be some special kind of paddle used to help propel a Durham boat from the stern.

161. "Bike" is a Scots term for the hive of bees, wasps or ants.

162. AB "bodys."

163. AB wrote "not" here.

164. AB "deameanure."

165. Curses.

by some mystic force and brought them sooner than they would have come without his blasphemous demonstration no one questioned him, all were pleased the help had come. However not time was lost in getting ashore the cable, ten yoke of oxen, and six horses in front. Everyone able to walk was ordered ashore but to keep the boat in sight.

Fain would I have gone with the rest, but being previously lost and the bumble bee sting of yesterday were[166] against me. No doubt their[167] anxiety lest[168] some mischanter should befall me it was decreed I was to remain onboard with the elderly women and children. Of course I was very much disappointed, but copious flow of tears and encouraged by the Captain who was now in his right mind again, that I was just the person he required to help him steer with the little rudder. Accordingly I was instructed in turning the lever of it in the same direction as he did the big splasher. The thought that I was of some importance was quite a solace to my wounded feelings and I have had the satisfaction of saying I was the only male passenger in the company that sailed up the long Sault except our two little brothers.

A powerful looking Negro drove the oxen. He appeared to be an adept at the business, walked back and forth to see that all pulled alike. He carried a long whip which he **[60]** used adroitly. It was impossible to hear a man's voice from the land, the current made a peculiar mur[mu]ring sound and the rippling of the water on the bows and sides of the boat as it ran by with great velocity prevented all communication by voice. The men ashore had some system of signaling to the Captain by waving their hands in different ways. Along the beach at irregular distances apart were posts, often quite a distance into the river. A lever much like a pump handle was fixed to the post but allowing it move easily up and down. I think this contrivance was to prevent the boat from being too far down in shore in a curve of slight bend in the river. When the cable got to the land side of the post the lever was lifted and the cable swung out. This job was performed by the boatmen. Often had to wade into the current up to the waist at the risk of being carried down the river, never again to wade the St. Lawrence.

The two men that drove the horses were tall grave looking men, fair specimens of the native American. They wore very high chip hats, which has been obsolete for many years, what shirts, light blue pants, neither vest nor coat. Had a good view of them when through the rapids. They had the appearance of men that knew their own business and no doubt were owners of the teams and natives of [New] York State. Not Yankees according to the American usage of the sobriquet. What remuneration for their services I never heard. I supposed, however they were employed and paid by the

166. AB "was."

167. AB "these."

168. AB "least."

Company to pull all their boats through the rapids. But how they knew to be at the place is still a mystery to me.

Have no distinct remembrance just when the rapids were passed only the river became very much wider. It was quite dark at [61] Ogdensburg[169] where we put up for the night. We then crossed to Prescott labouring with the long oars. Remember quite well on seeing the Wind Mill that became somewhat famous in Canadian history as the rendezvous of Von Shoults and his insurgents in 1838.

Riding the Steamer *Cobourg* from Prescott to Toronto

The Steamer *Cobourg*[170] came down the river and took the *Mary Ann* in tow, but how and in what way the passengers, luggage and other freight was transferred from the *Mary Ann* to the *Cobourg* my memory is blank. I think it must have been at Kingston. But I know it was Fare ye well old *Mary Ann* forever. It was quite dark at Kingston.

Can remember distinctly on the thousand Islands, the morning was quite foggy and the Steamer was anchored until the fog cleared away.

The Bay of Quinte was pointed out to our party by a Toronto merchant who was down getting goods. Among his freight was several large barrels of sugar, but it seems boys will be boys, in every age, country and condition of life. The Peterhead boys knew how to widen a space between the staves and insert a knife and lick without thought of breaking the eight[h] commandment. The Merchant was an Aberdeen man with the very orthodox Scotch name of Robert Mckay, or Mackie, as it was generally pronounced in Aberdeenshire. He had been looking around among his barrels, and discovered that thieves had been tampering with his sugar barrels. He was very angry, and threatened dire punishment if there was any more filching. But he could not watch his barrels continually, and every chance was improved to get a lick. He learned before he reached Toronto, that the men of the boat, one of them at least, was the principal delinquent, [62] for he caught him in the act, when the boys were asleep.

When looking from the steamboat towards the land, a dark line appeared, its volume increased or decreased according to distance. It was the forest line. It seemed to run parallel with the lakeshore. I do not think the boat called at any place along the lake except Cobourg and Port Hope, before arriving at Toronto. My father had acquaintances in the Township of Whitby, and was anxious to know about the locality, knew it was about thirty miles east of Toronto. One of the boat hands pointed it out, but there was nothing to distinguish it from the ordinary co[a]st line. There was no town there in 1835 do not think there was a wharf. Perry's Corners being

---

169. Ogdensburg is in New York State, on the south shore of the St. Lawrence, directly across the river from Prescott.

170. AB "Coburg" here and elsewhere.

the mart for the district around. Mr. Peter Perry being the principal businessman for many years. Think he was a member of the old parliament of Canada.

It was midday when the *Cobourg* was laid along side the wharf at Toronto. Still called York in the common phraseology of the people of town and country. Carts were in immediate attendance on the wharf to take our luggage to where our lodgings were to be for sometime. John Henderson and my father started away to look for a house as soon as the luggage was loaded on the carts leaving Mrs Henderson and my mother and the rest to follow. Before proceeding half way up the wharf a man presented himself in front of the first cart and demanded wharfage. My mother asked how much it was. He said a York shilling. Well how much was that, sevenpence half penny, or an English sixpence. This our first introduction to York money.

If I ever knew, I have entirely forgotten how the house was so easily found, as it was away up Lot[171] street, now Queen, fully one mile from the wharf. Of course, Yonge street wharf as at the [63] foot of Yonge Street, but there was Brown's wharf, and Gorries wharf,[172] which was east or west of Yonge Street, my memory is void. I think, however it was Yonge Street wharf that the *Cobourg* came alongside of. It was then a loose rickety affair, nothing like the wharfs at Montreal.

Back Stories of Chapter Seven

Bishop Alexander Macdonell

Bishop Alexander Macdonell (1762–1840) was born in Scotland, and became a something of a conservative power broker in the Canadas during the time of the 1837–38 Rebellion. As Uncle Alex noted, he was a very big man, although in his early seventies when Uncle Alex saw him. He was also a major conservative or Tory force at the time, even though he was involved with a bit of infighting with Anglican Tory stalwarts such as Bishop John Strachan.

Toronto When the Brodies First Arrived

Toronto when the Brodies first arrived can be described in several ways. For the aristocratic Anna Brownell Jameson, describing Toronto in the winter following the Brodies' arrival, deep in December, her first impression was as follows:

> What Toronto may be in summer, I cannot tell, they say it is

---

171. It was originally called Lot Street as there were large lots that went north from the street to Bloor. After the coronation of Queen Victoria in 1837 it was renamed.

172. This was another name for the Yonge Street wharf.

a pretty place. At present its appearance to me, a stranger, is most strangely mean and melancholy. A little ill-built town on low land, at the bottom of a frozen bay, with one very ugly church, without tower or steeple; some government offices, built of staring red brick, in the most tasteless, vulgar style imaginable; three feet of snow all around; and the gray, sullen, wintry lake, and the dark gloom of the pine forest bounding the prospect; such seems Toronto to me now (Jameson 1965: 17).

More charitably, it was a town on the move, growing rapidly. In 1824, it had a population of merely 1,685, increasing only slightly to 1,710 by 1830, but five years later it risen more than fivefold to 9,675. What was called the Home Districts around it (including the counties of York, Simcoe, Peel and surroundings) had literally multiplied (by more than four times) in size as well, from roughly 13,000 in 1820 to 58,308 in 1835 (Armstrong 1988: 34, 36).

Toronto was taking on the physical accoutrements of a city as well. Substantial red brick edifices were being erected on the main streets, including a city hall, a courthouse, the newly completed Chewett building at the southeast corner of King Street and York, and a fire hall. In 1833, the old wooden church was replaced by a statuesque stone structure of the St. James Cathedral. Aside from the early general stores, there were more specialist shops such as hardware, printing and publishing, silversmiths, bookstores, druggists, hatters, and a cigar store. And in the 1830s and 1840s taverns, from the elegant British Coffee House (a red brick establishment next to the Chewett Building) to the numerous shacks of convenience, sprung up everywhere (Armstrong 1988: 30–31). Mills and factories were also to be seen scattered across the town, including at least one brewery, distillery, and tannery.

Peter Perry

Peter Perry, born near Kingston, Ontario (1792–1851), was notable both in business and in politics. In the latter field he represented two different constituencies as a moderate reformer, first with the Legislative Assembly of Upper Canada (1824–36), and then the Legislative Assembly of the Province of Canada (1849–51). In business, he established a general store and built warehouses in what is today Whitby on the northern shore of Lake Ontario. One early name for that town was "Perry's Corners." Both as businessman and politician he pushed for the success of the natural harbour there and of a road connecting Whitby to Lake Scugog. The town at the end of that road is today known as Port Perry.

Chapter Eight
Life in Toronto in 1835 and the End of a Friendship

Our landlord was a jolly Yorkshire man Mr Luty or Lewty.[173] He was the owner of three dwel[l]ings in one building. He lived in one end we in the centre. Dr. Sybalds in the other end. Of this person more later[174] on. We had a fairly good habitation for about six weeks. Of course we were rather crowded, still got along very well. The back yard was the rendezvous for gossip. A crude shed on the back part of the yard was the receptacle[175] for wood, old barrels and every conceivable thing known as rubbish that could not be dumped on the street. At the back door or each dwelling (on one side) was a large rain barrel. A necessary convenience in those days, as today in more pretentious dwellings than Mr Lewty's. Having no furniture to occupy room down stairs, nor up stairs—both apartments[176] were fully utilized with the belongings of both families. Still it required no little ingenuity to meet the exigencies of the case without Jangle.[177]

Going to See William Lyon Mackenzie

My father having a letter of introduction from a Mr. Lowe a prominent gentleman of Aberdeen to W. L. Mackenzie asking him as a farmer to his friend the bearer to recommend him to a good part of the country to settle in, he Mr. Mackenzie being in the country a few years previous would be able to give valuable advice to a stranger. I accompanied my father to Mr. Mackenzie's office, in a small frame house on York Street. Mr Mackenzie read the letter and returned it. After asking a few **[64]** questions regarding family and means, recommended the Niagara district, the country around Hamilton, Brantford, and the County of York north of Toronto. The letter mentioned above I have in my possession, being a rather unique memento of over seventy years ago. Although the gray goose quil[l] "the mighty instrument of little men"[178] has been superseded by the modern steel pen, and gold fountain pen of still a later date, this letter proves that penman-

---

173. He was listed in the census of 1837 as "Leuty, Joseph, gentleman, 76 Lot st. W." (www.statictorontopubliclibrary.ca/da/pdfs/706129.pdf and Robertson, J. Ross, 1974: 139. By the time that the 1846–47 directory came out, the same property was owned by a Squire Moorhouse, who had it as a "provision store" (Robertson 1974: 281). Joseph Leuty was then living at 187 Queen Street West (Robertson 1974: 236)

174. AB "latter."

175. AB "receptable."

176. AB "appartments."

177. One traditional meaning of "jangle" in Scots is to complain loudly.

178. This is a quotation taken from a satirical poem by Lord Byron (see Back Stories in this chapter).

ship since the early thirties has not kept pace with the times. Mrs. Mackenzie hearing a Scotch voice, came out in the office. She inquired if any Scotch girls came out in the ship with him. She said "I am in need of a lass. I prefer a Scotch lass." My father told her he had charge of a young girl, daughter of a friend, thinking it might be a good place for Helen, he said, "I will speak to her, and send her down to speak to you. It is possible she may not like to be so far from us, we have no idea where we may settle yet." However the result was Helen was engaged as a domestic in the family of the man whose name became familiar (to English readers at least) all over the world in two years, and will go down in the history of Canada by one party politic as an honest man, a true patriot though mistaken in judgement, over zealous, aggravated[179] by the unmitigated abuse of the party in power. The Canadians of today are reaping the reward of intolerance of government by Family Compact. While the opposite party politic condemn him and his confederates as rebels, renegades and evil doers. Both parties are probably wrong in their deductions. No doubt the much needed reform would have come in time without rebellion. Still about every legitimate means had been used without effect. British Justice is beautiful in theory but rather slow to consummate. Lost all America to the British crown [65] now known as the United States of America.

Helen remained with the Mackenzies. I think over a year and a half. Of Mr. Mackenzie, she spoke of him as being a gentleman in every sense of the word, his hatred of malversation and snobbery amounted almost to a mania. The parting with Helen was sorrowful. But she knew a home was open for her whenever required. She had various experiences after this but ultimately became Mrs. Stephen Hubbard of the Township of Pickering.[180]

David Sinclair and my father started on a prospecting tour. John Macgillivray had gone to his Uncle in Whitby. Sandy Morrison still clung to us, seemed to have fallen in love with Betty. The Hendersons were looking out for something to do. In the meantime chum and I roamed abroad in quest of adventure. The old garrison and garrison (common) as it was called then was the scene of many of our peregrinations. Many wild flowers abounded, which were not native to the Giddle and Pinkie braes in the environment of Peterhead. Had we known the verse we might have quoted it:

---

179. AB "agravated."
180. See Back Stories in this chapter.

The Exile's Song – Robert Gilfillan[181]

The palm tree waveth high
And fair the myrtle springs.[182]
And to the Indian maid
The bulbul sweetly sings[183]
But I dinna see the broom[184]
We its tassels on the lee
Nor hear the linties[185] sing
O' my ain countree.

The Garrison Common[186]

What area there might have been in this common I could not venture an opinion. It was however a large tract. Some of it [**66**] had been originally a cedar swamp as many stumps were quite prevalent, but it was not wet for grass was abundant, and here and there where grass had not taken full possession many flowers were growing quite common in the woods of Ontario during the early settlements. I remember on hearing that the cedar that formed the stoc[k]ade around the old garrison was cut from this now common. It appears to me now that the present fair ground, and Central prison occupy part at least of what was part of the old common in 1835. And it may be the southwestern part of the city is built on it.

In 1835 it was a long walk from the Town proper to the garrison. Many of the town's people kept cows, and pastured them thro[u]gh the day on the common. The cows came down Lot street in the evening perhaps twenty or thirty in a row though not in close order. Threes, fours and sixes. Lately reading Mrs Agnes Mitchell's *[W]hen the [C]ows came Home* it brought to my remembrance lot street in a June evening in 1835.

---

181. This is the second stanza of the poem/song.

182. The family *Myrtaceae*, to which the various plants called "myrtle" belong, include a number of plants that would be considered "exotic" to a Scot (e.g., allspice, cloves and the eucalyptus).

183. The bulbul is a bird commonly found in many places in Africa, and in places in Asia. It is a bird that makes its presence known, as it is active and noisy.

184. The broom is a thorny shrub with yellow tassels. The word comes from an old Germanic term meaning "thorny shrub," and is cognate with the word "bramble." The household implement, the broom, was early made out of broom.

185. Linties are small finches, a Scots word for the linnet. The name derives from the bird's habit of eating flax seeds, the -lin- being cognate with linen and linseed, both of which come from the flax plant.

186. The Garrison Common is the land immediately surrounding Fort York, west of Bathurst. There is a park there now smaller than the original Common.

[When the Cows Come Home – Agnes Mitchell – 1891[187]]
With jingle, jangle jingle,[188]
Soft sounds[189] that sweetly mingle,
The cows are coming home;
Malvine, and Pearl, and Florimel
DeKamp, Redrose, and Gretchen Schell
Queen Bess, and Sylph, and Spangled Sue
Across the fields I hear her loo loo
And clang her silver bell.
Go-ling, go-lang, golinglelingle
With faint far sounds that mingle,
The cows come slowly home
And with [mother]-songs of long-gone years,
And with baby joys, and childish tears,
And youthful hopes, and youthful fears,
When the cows come home.

I do not mean to insinuate the cows in 1835 had more sense than cows generally have in 1906, else I might be treading on a different theme from the purport of my narrative, but I will say this however. Laying aside the law of evolution that the cows I refer to each one knew her owner's house and drew up at **[67]** front door and complacently chewing her cud and gave her milk to maid or matron without any trouble. What they did with their cows during the night I do not know, but they all started back again in the morning in much the same order as they came in the evening.

Chum and I often went up to the garrison to see the soldiers drill. On Sunday mornings we made a point to be up in time to see the regiment form and march down to the Church of England the band playing as they marched. Only a few of them went into the church, but all were ready to form at the church door when the service was over. It was a small frame building, would be considered a small church at present even in a rural village. Still it had some pretention to high churchism. It had a kind of gallery and other little fixings to indicate, I am the Church of England. It stood on the same site as St. James' now stands. It was burned down over sixty years ago.[190] And another far larger and up to date edifice was built on the same site. I can remember nothing of the officiating clergyman but supposed he must have been Bishop Strachan.

Somewhere in the vicinity of the garrison in 1835 there was a saw-

---

187. Little information is available online about the poet, other than publication of the lines of this one poem.

188. This is the second stanza of a longer poem.

189. Uncle Alex used "tones."

190. This was in the Great Fire of 1849.

mill.[191] Chum and I after great labour and perseverance succeeded in extracting a large slab[192] from a pile at one end of the mill near the tail race. We managed to float it down to the bay having flat side down, we roll'd up <u>oor</u> breeks sat straddle one at each end and with our hands paddled down to the first wharf. There was nothing in the way. Everything is now so changed I can not tell whether it was Yonge Street wharf or not. The topographer [68] of seventy years ago, viewing the same place would come to the conclusion he had never been there before.

Alexander Henderson: A Former Chum

John Henderson being a cooper by trade got employment making flour barrels for a large flouring mill on the Humber about eight miles west of Toronto. The family moved there and I lost my chum. To be brief about the sequel of the Henderson family. After going through various experiences of coopering, and farming, they final[l]y settled down in Toronto as merchants. My Chum did fairly well, and became Alderman Henderson. He became quite pompous in manner, dress and style of speech. Turned his back on old acquaintances,[193] even come even refused to countenance people who came later from the same town (Peterhead), and although he could hardly do otherwise than give me a very little countenance with a sickly smile when I met him in Toronto, or happened to call into his store, which was on my way out of town. His demeanour indicated there was a great gulf between us, that my company was unsavoury to him was quite palpable. There was not need of this snobbery on his part. He was known in the school lingual in Peterhead, <u>Sawaky Henerson</u>. Now a civic ruler, and important business man in the Capital of the Banner province in the Dominion of Canada wearing the insignia of his importance in broad cloth, and mincing airs on the street. To prosper in business. To become even wealthy by judicious management, and be placed in position of trust and influence by our fellow men, is highly commendable and should be esteemed. But attained for self importance, self aggrandizement accompanied by inordinate pride and vanity becomes nauseating and portrays an infinitesimal[194] soul. Of course he knew well not to go beyond certain point in superlative eminence for he doubtless was aware [69] that I held the trump card in the game of family independence. His father was completely strapped on arrival at Quebec. It was my father's money that brought the Hendersons to Toronto. In repaying that money it came like paying for a dead horse. I remember the last instalment was a churn, and two pails which in primitive

191. This would probably be by the Humber River, where there were several sawmills at this time.

192. AB "slabe."

193. AB "acquantenances."

194. AB "infitismal."

appearance might have been coeval with Jacob's ring-streaked and grizzled cows.¹⁹⁵ His brothers flourished for a few years "like a green bay tree"¹⁹⁶ then blighted and left Toronto under a cloud for the land of the free.

Alexander Henderson was not only a native of the same Town as myself but attended the same school and in the same class up to the day before sailing. Although not ranked among the brightest boys in the class, he was seldom far down. Never knew him to be at the head. He was not one of my boon companions while at school, but became so onboard the *Alert*, and continued to be my chum on the whole journey up to parting in Toronto, having no secrets one from the other. So far as I remember we never quarreled. He was not a favourite¹⁹⁷ among the sailors on account of his intolerable impudence.

Destiny is a curious thing. The boy of eight or nine years of age may not always be indicative of the man to be. There was no remarkable difference between Alexander Henderson and Myself mentally or physically only he was fair, and I was dark, he was in truth my antithesis. His hair was red as a carrot, mine as black as ebony. As a rule he was generally below me in the class, the three boys who were evidently the brightest scholars in the class, Charley Wallace, Joseph Wallace, and James Mcleod, I have been told never got above being journeyman tailors. But **[70]** Sandy Henderson had a trait of character that made up for other deficiencies in his make up, that carried him through a dilemma that I at least did not possess, a stock of unmitigated impudence. This vice, virtue, or unmannerly conduct¹⁹⁸ occasionally got him into serious trouble and distress.

Johnny MacGillivray when a lad had the misfortune of being severely hurt by the couping¹⁹⁹ of a cart. A wheel passed over his face crushing his nose. In healing it grew to an abnormal size, not so much in width, but stood out from the plane of his face like the jib boom of a large ship. The sailors called it his cutwater. Although they indulged in launching little witticisms about Johnny's cutwater, they according to sailor generosity hated to hear or see any allusion to Johnny's nose going beyond a certain point. Now my chum seemed to take a special delight to mimic Johnny's hi'land²⁰⁰ accent and caricature his nose. He had been reproved and warned to desist many times, but he took no heed to warning. One day he made a paper nose as like Johnny's as possible and as Johnny was pacing the deck in a

195. AB "ring straiked and grizzled." This is a reference to Jacob's cows in Genesis (30:32–4, 31:7, 31:10 and 31:12).

196. Psalm 37:35: "I have seen the wicked in great power, and spreading himself like a green bay-tree."

197. AB "favourate."

198. AB "conduck."

199. This means falling or turning over.

200. That is, "highland."

pensive mood, he sneaked up behind him with the paper nose stuck on his own proboscis. Hoggie seeing the act slipped up behind him and gave him a kick on an unmentionable part of the body that sent him squabbling in the head scuppers[201], by the impetus of the kick. Hoggies souwester fell off. Chum seized the souwester and threw it overboard. Quick as thought Hoggie grabbed Chum's bonnet, and getting a piece of wood from the carpenter fixed it in the crown, to keep it afloat. Set up a mast and rigged stunsails,[202] and lowered it overboard. Not a member of the Henderson family interfered. Captain, Cabin passenger,[203] passengers and sailors looked on amusedly. The bonnet bobbed away astern and was [71] soon lost in the distance. For a day or two chum had no bonnet nor cap, but the cabin passenger more through the ludicrous than benevolence procured a piece of canvas and some oakum and fabricated a cap, or hat, or bonnet, for him. In shape it partook of no particular type of hat then in existence.[204] It might in one single feature [have] resembled an old fashioned night cap having a top. Here the likeness ceased for the top was stuffed with oakum. There never was such another cap as this since the Fall of Man, and never will there be such another cap seen like this one to the end of time. He was this caricature during the remainder of the voyage.

Alexander Henderson no doubt showed himself to be the wiser boy of the two on many occasions. At school if there was any cause for a fight, Chum was not there. If there was a <u>pullback</u>, a game some like the tug of war, only instead of a rope each boy locked his hands round the other's middle and pulled, each side trying to pull the other over a scratch across the street. Never saw chum in a pull. Not all the jibs[205], scoffs, lubber and white livered coward by the sailors could induce him to follow me up to the crosstrees of the mainmast of the *Alert*. He knew well there was nothing to be gained by endangering himself when there was nothing to be gained.

Well now comes the destined part of our lives. Why was I to be a farmer, to chop, log, help to clear up a farm, away in the back woods in my youthful years. Subjected to the turmoil incidental to pioneer life? The vicissitudes of cold winters and hot summers, and the hardships attendant on a farm after the woods have been cleared away, for many years.

The time when there were[206] mowing machines, no reapers, [72] no

---

201. Scuppers are holes through which water will drain to the outside.

202. Also called "studding sails," these are extra sails added to the mainsail to increase sail area.

203. The distinction was between cabin passenger and what would later be called steerage. The passengers that took the latter option were more numerous, and saved a good deal of money.

204. AB "existance."

205. AB "gibs."

206. AB "was."

binders, no drills, no cultivators, not even a horserake. No hayloaders, no horse forks, nor slings. The cradle, reaping hook, and scythe did all the cutting of grain and hay. Then there were[207] the weary days of raking and binding often getting the fingers paved with thistles. Load and unload with the ubiquitous pitch fork, frequently by the side of a shed, forcing the hay into a small hole and the mercury away up in the nin[e]ties. It may be urged that there was not near so much haying and harvesting to do as there is now. Admitted not on the aggregate, but years before there was a machine worthy of the name, many farms in the County of York had all cleared except a ten or twelve acres left for firewood, on a hundred acre farm.

There is much said and written (now-a-days) about boys and girls leaving the farm for city life, on account of the hard and drudgery work, and many plans, and much advice have been suggested to keep them on the farm. Well what of the boys when I was a boy? When I look back and reflect on those by-gone[208] years, and the physical labour performed by the first settlers up to the fifties, it is a marvel that half of them did not die prematurely from sheer decrepitude. But they did not die sooner than they do now, proving hard work will kill no one, providing it be done judiciously. But it may be very unsavoury to a youth who knows this Quondam[209] Chum is having a much better time.

Far away from the cheering gleam of city life was I, when my old chum was in his store dressed in broad cloth and fine linen apparently enjoying so many blessings to which I was a stranger. It has often passed through my mind [that] had my father remained in Toronto, and engaged in some business (say storekeeping) how our future as a family **[73]** might have been. I have heard our departed friend George Bruce[210] aver, and he was a man of [a]cute observation and keen perception, that as a rule men and women found the place in this life they were best adapted to fill. That it was a philosophical fact as true as small gravel would pass through the messes of a riddle[211] and large to stay in. That the many Hamdens and inglorious Miltons[212] was simply a poet's fancy. Be this as it may, what the Fates have in store for us from nine years to middle age and death remains unanswered and no doubt is wisely hidden from our ken. Still the query remains unanswered. Was my chum only fit to be a city merchant and civic rule, and

207. AB "was."

208. AB "bye gone."

209. This is Latin for "former."

210. He was probably referring to the Scottish born George Bruce (1781–1866) who came to America, revolutionized the printing business, and was something of a public figure.

211. A riddle is a large mesh or coarse sieve often used to sift soil, taking out such items as small stones, twigs, and lumps of clay.

212. See the entry for Thomas Gray in Back Stories for this chapter.

I fit for nothing but a clod hopper. My old chum has gone over the great majority many years ago. What he left to his family as inheritance or to the wisdom of the Aldermanic posterity of Toronto I never heard.

Dr. Sybalds and His Miracle Cholera Cure

Dilating at greater length than I intended when I began on the Henderson family I had almost forgotten Dr. Sybalds of whom I have already mentioned. He was a tall man. In fact elongation appeared to be the contour of his personality. His face was long and thin, naturally pale, which was intensified in appearance by large piercing[213] dark eyes, as if to sift you through before you had spoken to him. A heavy mustache[e] extending around almost to his ears as black as Erebus.[214] He was the first man I had ever seen with a mustach[e]. Mustaches were rarely worn in 1835. It was taken for granted by the ordinary class of people that a man wearing a mustache[e] was either demented or at least very fain to exhibit himself as a rara avis[215] among his fellow men. Just what was the Dr's motive for wearing this appendage on his upper lip when it was so uncommon, very likely he thought [74] it was nobody's business. It may be he saw through a vista of years the coming fashion and posed as a leader. He introduced himself to my mother as a graduate from the Royal Medical College, Edinburgh. Passed an examination in London, and received a number of letters to his name indicative of his wonderful skill as a Physician. He said Jesus Christ appeared to him during the cholera plague of 1831-2-3, and told him to prepare a cure for the cholera. He had faith in the revelation, prepared the Elixir, went down to the hospital and administered it to patients already given up to death by attendant Drs. In two or three days he had them, a hundred men walking up the street that should have been dead. Some of them a little sallow—but effectually cured of cholera morbus. These men should have been dead and buried according to the diagnosis of the hospital Drs. He charged them with persecution of him that the patients he claimed to have cured were already convalescent before he administered his elixir. That in every way possible they strove to rob him of his God given knowledge. He spoke with great volubility the froth working out from the sides of his mouth. He said he was going home to Britain in the fall to expose the perfidy of the rascally Drs that had wrought his ruin to the Home government. Parties who knew this peculiar man in better days said he had been badly used by the medical faculty of the time. He had been an extensive reader, and student of history ancient and modern, had a large library of what he called standard works on the medical profession.

On a board above his door was painted in large letters, Sybald's Elixir

---

213. AB "peircing."
214. Erebus was the ancient Greek god who was the personification of darkness.
215. Latin: "rare bird."

of life or Universal medicine. A few people called on him apparently of the poorer class, but we never saw him go [75] out professionally. How he made a living for himself and family was a query. His son a lad of 16 or 18 years, went down to the wharf occasionally and did something in a warehouse. Two girls perhaps ten and twelve years old, were fairly well endowed mentally and physically, nothing observable to connect them with their father's dementia. They did not go to school, yet were excellent scholars. Spoke the purest of English. My mother thought he had taught them himself, for he was too much of a Misanthrope to trust them with any teacher. Mother and Betty were very anxious to know something of his wife, but on this subject both him and the girls were mute.

This strange di[s]ciple of Esculpious[216] might have passed as having a hobby that he rode unmercifully at certain times, but he would gallop over the same course every day to the boys in the back yard if he got the chance. The saying of Festus to Paul would not have been inappropriate to this curious man of healing.[217]

Back Stories of Chapter Eight

William Lyon Mackenzie

William Lyon Mackenzie (1795–1861) was a controversial major political and journalistic figure in Canadian politics during the 19th century. He was born near Dundee, Scotland, roughly 100 miles south of Alexander Brodie's birthplace. Mackenzie was raised by a single mother from the time he was three weeks old, and came to Canada in 1820. His journalistic career was early centred around *The Colonial Advocate*, of which he was the editor and owner from 1824. From the start he used it as a tool for criticizing what was called the Family Compact, a close-knit group of Tory leaders who held and abused tremendous power in what was then called Upper Canada. They used means both legal and illegal, violent and non-violent to suppress his highly vocal and active opposition.

He was elected and served in the 10th Parliament of the Legislative Assembly of Upper Canada in 1829, and was elected again in 1831. The Tory-controlled Legislative Assembly successfully voted to expel him for his opposition, but Mackenzie was re-elected almost unanimously by the electorate in a by-election in January 1832. Another motion was passed to expel him shortly thereafter, but again he won by a landslide in a second by-election. Later that year, the same thing happened again, repeated twice more the next year. In 1834 he was elected the first mayor of the newly

---

216. A(e)sculapius was the ancient Greek god of medicine.

217. I suspect that he meant to allude to the line from Luke 4:23—"Physician, heal thyself"—which had nothing to do with either Festus or Paul.

incorporated city of Toronto, a position he held until the next year. In 1835 he was elected to the 13th Parliament of Upper Canada, but lost the next year.

He early on became a major leading figure in the developing rebellion that began in open form in 1837. A few days after the Battle at Montgomery's Tavern, he escaped to Buffalo in the United States, and declared his intention to establish an independent republic in Canada. In an American trial held in June 1839 he was sentenced to 18 months imprisonment, to be pardoned by the American president in May 1840. He did not return to Canada until 1849, after the passing of an amnesty bill concerning the rebellion earlier that year. He was re-elected to the next Legislature in 1851 and served until he resigned in 1858. He died in 1861.

Helen Ellen Miller

Helen Ellen Miller (1819–87) was around the age of 16 when she went to work for the Mackenzies. After she left the Mackenzies, she would soon marry a Stephen Hubbard (1805–1883) and go to live in Pickering, to the east of Toronto. They would have eight children, five girls and three boys. The second oldest child was born in 1840, so she probably married in her late teens when her husband was in his mid-thirties.

George Gordon Byron

George Gordon Byron, usually known as Lord Byron (1788–1824), wrote a very long satirical poem lampooning writers and composers of song lyrics. In the second stanza we have these lines:

> O' Nature's noblest gift my grey goose quill
> Slave of my thoughts, obedient to my will
> Torn from thy parent bird to from a pen
> The mightiest instrument of little men.

Robert Gilfillan

Robert Gilfillan (1798–1850) was a popular Scottish poet and songwriter. Although he wrote "The Exile's Song," he himself never left his native land, not even for England.

Thomas Gray

Thomas Gray (1716–71) was a poet most famous for his "Elegy Written in a Country Churchyard." He is referred to by Uncle Alex with his mention of "Hampden" and "Miltons":

> Some village Hampden that with dauntless breast
> The little tyrant of his fields withstood

Some mute inglorious Miltons here may rest.
Some Cromwell guiltless of his country's blood.

John Hampden (1594–1643) was a leader in the Parliament that overthrew Charles I. Oliver Cromwell (1599–1658) was the leader of the Commonwealth that took over after Charles I was overthrown, and John Milton (1608–1674) was a noted poet as well as a civil servant in the Commonwealth. Gray was suggesting that the potential for talent for leadership and poetry can sometimes lie undiscovered because of fortune. Uncle Alex was arguing for a kinder view of destiny.

Alexander Henderson

A biography of Alexander Henderson (1824–1887) can be found in the *Dictionary of Canadian Biography*, an indication of his significance in his time. The author of the piece, Daniel James Brock, had read Uncle Alex's memoir, and used it quite extensively, although not so much the negative parts. After Henderson sold the family dry goods business, he became heavily involved in the growing real estate market in Toronto. From there he became a politician, serving as a city alderman from 1868 to 1876. Later "chum" served as a justice of the peace (Daniel James Brock, "Henderson, Alexander [1824–87]," in *Dictionary of Canadian Biography*, vol. 11, University of Toronto/Université Laval, 2003–, accessed April 10, 2018, http://www.biographi.ca/en/bio/henderson_alexander_1824_87_11E.html).

St. James Cathedral

There have been four Anglican or Church of England churches on the site of 65 Church Street at King. It is Toronto's oldest congregation. The first one was constructed of wood in 1807 and damaged by American invaders during the Battle of York. It was replaced in 1831 by a larger structure built of stone, opening in 1832. It burned down in 1839. The next church was constructed the same year, but then burned down in 1849. The fourth and final one was completed in 1853, the delay owing to needed funding, with the famous tower added.

Chapter Nine
Finding a Home and Settling In

To resume my narrative, I must turn back in order to connect it with a previous omission. My father visited his friends in Whitby before acting on Mackenzie's recommendation. There was a farm for sale there quite suitable in every way except immediate[218] possession, this in my father's view was quite important. There was a small house and an acre or two chopped, but the title[219] and possession could not be obtained for at least a year.

After spending a week in Whitby and Pickering they returned to Toronto, David Sinclair and my father. They then turned their attention towards Mackenzie's suggestion. They did not proceed very far in the Niagara district, but prospected principally around Hamilton, Brantford, and the Township of Esquesing. Did not find a farm just suitable, they came back, and turned to the country north [76] [of] Toronto. The country south of Hamilton and Brantford especially had the reputation of being specially subject to fever and ague else there was excellent land in the Valley of the Grand River.

They proceeded north as far as Barrie, went up Yonge Street to the Holland [Land]ing. Spent a few days looking round in the townships a[d]jacent to Lake Simcoe. Went as far as Coldwater, the Narrows and Orillia. I think they were also at Penetanguishene. Not finding just what they wanted they were returning to Whitby by way of Newmarket through Whitchurch and Pickering, to ascertain if a house could be obtained to take the family to until possession could be given of the farm in view.

After crossing the Ridges by an angling road through the woods to the fifth concession[220] (in after years) they came to a place[221] with a small clearing, small log house, and very small log barn, fence around the little clearing sown, an open common. Everything dilapidated and in a ruinous condition, but the soil was good, and the locality quite desirable. On leaving this place to proceed on their way to Whitby, they came to an old man splitting rails by the roadside. They inquired about the farm they had seen. The old man informed them it was for sale, was owned by a Church of England Minister, who lived at Thornhill on Yonge Street, and he believed he had given it to his daughter and understood she was anxious to sell, as the man who had this place so many years to clear so many acres, fence it,

---

218. AB "immeadiate" here and elsewhere.

219. AB "tittle" here and elsewhere.

220. This is fifth concession in Whitchurch Township, now a northern extension of Warden, with the part that connects with the farm being a dead end street (not making it to Stouffville Road) named Warden Lane.

221. It is on the west side of the road.

and otherwise keep the place form depreciating in value. Instead of doing as agreed upon, he sold timber, cut great notches in the maple in the sugar bush to make them run mores sap. In short despoiled every thing he could and cleared out.

Instead of going on to Whitby they turned towards Toronto by [77] way of Thornhill and bought the farm. Made arrangements with Mr. Mortimer[222] and Daughter when to meet in Toronto and get the Deed and transfer made over. The price of a first class bush farm with a small clearing on it, perhaps no more than the settling duty, I might say that the first start, was in the locality mentioned from six to ten dollars an acre according to quality and other conveniences. My father paid one thousand dollars in sovereigns[223] for the farm now known as Cragie Burn farm of gold medal celebrity.[224] I might say just here that the County of York was about half settled in this locality to the south. On the north there were[225] only two clearings on the fifth concession line or road allowance, for six miles.

Well after a hurried packing up again, buying glass, putty, nails and many other necessities to make the house a kind of habitable , also provision for a few days. Three wagons appeared one morning, and as usual on such occasions, after much lifting and pushing and changing of positions, in the wagons, were loaded and a start was made. Of course there were good byes to the few neighbors and friends we had made in our short stay in Toronto. With many kind invitations to come and see them whenever we came to the city. But lo and behold the addition to our family without adoption, Sandy Morrison came along. I have not a very vivid remembrance of the road from first impressions. Have heard Yonge Street was stoned or Macadamized[226] as far as Yorkville, or what became Yorkville in after years. Remember there was a toll gate at this place and the old man driving the wagon we elder boys were in, said we were one mile and a quarter from Lot street (now Queen). Yorkville was away outside the City limits and for many years an Incorporated Village.[227] It was taken into the City a few years ago. Few of the streets in Toronto were macadamized in [78] 1835 and pine stumps were no great novelty in the newer streets. As far west as Mr Lewty's it was no uncommon thing to see a man or woman

222. Rev. George Mortimer (1784–1844). See Back Stories in this chapter.

223. AB "soverigns."

224. In 1890, the farm, then owned by the baby of the family, Charles John Brodie (1834–1909) was awarded a gold medal from the Ontario Department of Agriculture, the only one of the entrants to win that high honour; others won silver or bronze. See Back Stories in this chapter.

225. AB "was" here and elsewhere.

226. See Back Stories in this chapter.

227. During the 1960s it was known as "the Village," and was the scene for music and for showing off how cool you were. At least that was the way I saw it.

come out in the morning with an axe and hack a few chips from a nearby stump to kindle their fire to cook the morning repast. In a few minutes the odour of frying was perfuming the sidewalk where there was one. From my future knowledge of stumps and kindling fires I have no doubt those were pine stumps. Evidently there had been large pines growing to the west of the city sometime.

At Hoggs Hollow[228] the road ran away to the east of the milldam then skirted around the banks of the Don River, coming out on the straight road again near where Vanostrand's store[229] used to be. As it was the beginning of July there was no deep mud but many deep ruts that had been cut by wagon wheels when the road was soft earlier in the season. Pieces of corduroy[230] were frequent in what was in 1835 perhaps the greatest thoroughfare in Upper Canada. We three elder boys were in the last wagon. We got off many times, and ran along the road to look at something we had never see before.

We have imported a dog and a bitch from Peterhead. The dog was named Gelert after Llewellyn's peerless hound,[231] the bitch after the old woman we got her from whose sobriquet was Wadie all over the town. Why she got the name of Wadie Robb, Robb being her surname, I never heard. Pretentious names to dogs are a good deal like pretentious names to the human genera, seldom ever do they do honour to the prototype. Our Gelert did not possess any of the noble qualities of his predecessor. The only redeeming quality he had if it could be called a quality was a peaceful disposition and an appetite so voracious that he ate anything or everything that came in his way. Whether through this abnormal appetite or some other of the ills that dogs are heir to [79] I cannot say, being ignorant on dog distemper, however he got very sick, and after being dosed with sulphur several times and no sign of convalescence he was given up as Drs

---

228. James Hogg, a Scot, came to the area (centred around York Mills/Wilson and Yonge Street) in 1824, and developed a successful whisky distillery and grist mill. It wasn't named Hoggs Hollow until his sons John and William divided up the land in 1856.

229. Cornelius Van Nostrand had fought in the American Revolution as a British officer. He moved onto a lot on Yonge Street in 1805. His grandson Cornelius was in the York militia in the War of 1812. One or the other owned a grist mill and saw mill in Hoggs Hollow, and for a while owned the Gold Lion Inn/Hotel which was slightly north of what is now the Highway 401 bridge, on the west side of Yonge Street.

230. This refers to logs that are placed at a 90 degree angle to the street, having the ridged effect of corduroy.

231. In the story of Gelert, Prince Llewellyn of Wales returns from hunting to find his baby son missing and blood on the muzzle of Gelert. Incorrectly assuming that Gelert had killed his son, he slays the dog. He then finds the missing child alive and a wolf lying dead who had attacked the child. The dying yelp of Gelert is said in the story to have haunted the Prince for the rest of his life. This story is the subject of poetry that Uncle Alex would have read, notably *Beth Gelert or The Grave of the Greyhound*, by the English poet William Robert Spencer (1769–1834).

say, and shot. Wadie through some unknown cause to local dog Physicians at least to those men and neighbors who professed to have skill in dog diseases, lost the faculty of her hind quarters, and trailed them around for at least one year. Many cures were advised but none applied, when wonderful to tell, without any antidote whatever, she recovered the use of her hind quarters again, so that she could run with a kind of junkety jink motion, and when she got or rather chanced to get a pig by the ear, she would not let go until choked.[232] Her conduct became unbearable. A whelp (or as they were called in Peterhead a <u>folp</u> was raised from her which promised fair for sometime to redeem the reputation of his mother, and uncle perhaps a hundred times removed. He was also named Gelert, but he walked in the way of his father and committed grievous offences against the morality of dogs generally which caused his premature death. Also great many propositions as to the most human method of executing Wadie. It was finally agree to coax her down to the woods and hang her. We had no knowledge of the science of hanging. Never thought of the weight of the body, and the length of the drop, to correspond with it. We made no allowance for this most important sequence[233] in the case of hanging as duly considered by Ratcliffe[234] and other successful hangman. We simply got the noose round her neck, the end of the rope over the limb of a tree and pulled. When clear of the ground, her stifled yells were so piteous that Jamie and I who were the hangmen ran home and left poor Wadie to die a most ignominious death. Her eyes seem to implore us [80] for mercy, and say, "what have I done to merit a death like this. I have done nothing but followed the instinct of my nature as all my race have done before me." So ended our success in dog importations, and breeding of dogs. Well if dogs have ghosts, and have any cause to come back and chide those who have ill used them in this life, it is wonderful Wadie did not appear to Jamie and I whenever we approached the place of her bungled execution. But she did not come back. But like Llewellyn of old when we passed the fatal tree where she hung for months like the worst of criminals, we thought her dying yell resounded through the woods.

    I have digressed again, but to come back to where I left off we had to attend to these dogs. We could not keep them on the wagon all the time, and were afraid for losing them on the road. They were very sensible with other dogs they met, and seemed anxious to fraternize with them.

    On the road were pigs, sheep, cows, and even a horse occasionally and nobody herding them was a marvel to us. To see two pigs lying together in a mud hole right in the middle of the road, was one of the seven wonders

232. AB "chocked."

233. AB "secquence"

234. John Robert Radclive (also known as Ratcliffe' 1856-1911) was Canada's first professional executioner, serving that function from 1892–99, hanging at least 69 people.

to us. No doubt we annoyed the old teamster but he kept his temper, even seemed to enjoy our remarks on objects new to us in pure Buchan Doric.

The teamsters fed their horses at Thornhill and we ate our lunch. After leaving Thornhill I have no distinct recollection of the road, only the signs on some of the Taverns as we passed. There was the Victory in full sail (Lord Nelson's flag ship), Sir Thomas Picton on horse back, The Enniskillen[235] Dragoon until we came to Richmond Hill. After entering the Township of Markham, new scenes, different styles of houses, and different barns attracted our attention. Here and there an old old style cider press, great beams of timber looked to us like starting to build a ship, but where was the water to launch her into. Here we saw the first man and woman [81] in Dutch costume or more properly speaking the costume of the Tunkers and Men[n]onites. In the County of York they were generally called Dunkards and Menese [?] among themselves. The dress was so like that worn by the German people that came over to England and Scotland every summer. Went through the streets selling little brooms, singing the song of buy a broom, that on the first sight of them Geordie called out, "O' see the broomies."

On the fourth concession nearly one mile and a quarter north of the four corners, Reid's [C]orners, now Victoria Square, the front wagon stuck fast in a hole opposite a farm house. The farmer and his wife seeing the trouble and taking in the situation at a glance came out to give what assistance they could. During the time the men were occupied getting the wagon out the woman and my mother had become friends. Sympathy seldom fails in being a passport to the heart. The name of this family is Foot. They had come from England the previous summer, and knew the experience of the Durham boats. The friendship begun that summer afternoon never ceased as long as the elder members of the families were alive.

The wagons stopped a few minutes at a blacksmith's shop on the Townline and the Smith and his wife came out with much gush and demonstration of fraternity.

We arrived at the long looked for place at last, well over in the afternoon. The teamsters found some old troughs and fed their horses, while the wagons were unloading. We ran over the clearing chasing sheep, pigs, and cows, but they disregarded our proprietorship, and acted towards us as if possession to them was the main point in ownership as they had undisputed possession for several years. A few gooseberry, raspberry and black [82] cap bushes growing in the remains of a half burned log heap attracted our attention, and the anticipation of berries without stint was a solace in the meantime to future bliss.

Our home was not one of the most primitive dwellings in some respects. It really had some pretentions to a higher class structure than its

---

235. A more likely spelling is Inniskilling.

compeers in the neighborhood. It had what was called a stoop, sometimes a porch, now with more elaborate architecture frenchified into <u>Verandah</u>. It had an upstairs, properly speaking up a rude ladder occasionally it was called the <u>laft</u>.[236] But here all pretentions to style ceased. The roof was three quarter boards, and slabs laid on the cracks. This seems all right in words, or in theory, but the result was, the boards sag[g]ed in the middle not being properly supported, leaving many open spaces for rain and snow to come in. There was no window to lighten the attic only what came through the cracks in the roof and gable. In so far as ventilation was concerned, I am inclined to believe that the science of ventilation of today has not been much improved since the plan and architecture of our old house was approved. Although it was all that was required for pure air it as very uncomfortable. Every shower of rain that come went through the roof as through a sieve. There was a rush to place dishes on the beds to protect them from being soaked through. This was trouble enough in the day, but in the night was very troublesome indeed. In winter the snow drifted through every crack and cran[n]y forming kaleidoscope wreaths on our beds and floor of the attic. This was not as bad as the rain as it could be swept up and carried out before thawing. We used to undress at the fire in winter all but shirt and drawers and run up the ladders and into bed as quick as possible. Father by some means cut a hole in the west gable,[237] and **[83]** inserted a six by nine [inch] pane of glass, to give us a little more light. It was [of] no particular benefit, except on Sunday mornings in summer when there was no work to hurry us up. We could like and philosophize on the skill of the mud wasps as they built their clay cells and deposited an egg and spider in each cell as food for their larvae until they came out a full fledged wasp ready to fly and perform the amenities of mud wasp life to death like every other creature. Mud wasps have all but disappeared from old Ontario, and sought places more congenial to their nature. New houses and close[d] attics have deprived them of places to fill great nature's plan.

Our attic was not a first class sleeping apartment, notwithstanding its ventilating advantage. It became a kind of hospital for boots, and shoes, that had suffered from injuries consequent to their duty, and not unlikely constitutional disabilities of various kinds. At certain seasons it became a rendezvous for cats. At other times rats and mice held high carnival enough to scare old Morpheus[238] from the Attic forever. Especially was this the case during a Caterwauling. If such orgies were enacted for one single night in

---

236. This is probably an archaic form of "loft."

237. AB "gabble."

238. Morpheus was the ancient Greek god of dreams.

a present day young man's bedchamber in the east Riding of Middlesex[239] there certainly [would] be a veritable crisis, to say nothing of bed bugs as the Negro[240] said they were all married boys and had large families. But boys in North York seventy years ago who were all day in the field, in the woods, in the chopping logging wearied with toil learned by experience to sleep in defiance of cats, rats, mice bugs, and apparitions of old boots, shoes, broken dishes, and many curios that might have delighted Captain O'Grose.[241]

There was no compartment below in the house. I think it was 18 x 24, Mother's bed in one corner a trundle bed that could be pushed **[84]** under during the day, for the younger members of the family. Modesty was just as genuine in pioneer days as today, but the pioneer hous[e]keeper was often at her wit's end to improvise to accom[m]odation in hospitality to visitors from a distance, or a casual wayfarer. On such occasions a bed had to be spread on the floor. It could not be otherwise. For drawingrooms, parlours, dining[242] rooms, bed chambers, with all their paraphernalia of furniture, carpets, and many things too tedious to mention. Organs and Pianoforte were still in contemplation among pioneer folk in 1835. All looked forward to a time when troubles and inconveniencies would be emancipated in a grand new house. Many of them lived to realize this anticipated bliss, but according to their own confessions it is a question whether the realiz[at]ion was wholly unaduler[at]ed as hoped for.

We lived for three years in the house before it was shingled or a partition put across forming a kitchen and small room which served as a kind of parlour and bedroom, the five boys having full control of the attic. Previous to this we had a large box stove to heat the end of the house furtherest from the fire.

In this house we lived fifteen years. Only had a Dr. called once in that time in a case of scarlet fever. If there was one thing more than another that caused us serious inconvenience it was the lack of sufficient light. Only two small windows, six by nine glass, one on the end directly opposite the fire place, the other close [to] the side of the door which was to one side of the centre of the house. So in a dark day it was not a cheerful aspect inside.

My nar[r]ative is growing too long and may not be very interesting to young people of today, but as my thoughts dwell on the long ago incidents, for years laid up in my memory's **[85]** come forth and I cannot refrain from

---

239. Uncle Alex was referring here to the place where his Dorchester farm was at the time of his writing this manuscript. He might have had a particular grandson in mind when he wrote this.

240. It is possible that Uncle Alex obtained this saying after reading a copy of the then popular work by Joel Chandler Harris (1848–1908), *Uncle Remus: His Songs and Sayings* (1881).

241. See Back Stories in this chapter (Francis Grose).

242. AB "dinning."

telling them even at the risk of boring my young friends to some degree, but it must be remembered my story is of old times.

It was not a very refreshing sleep we got in our new home the first night. It had to undergo a thorough renovation by scraping and scrubbing, and all the means within our power in sanitary[243] efficiency[244] before beds could be a[d]justed for the night. And notwithstanding all the purification possible there was an odour exceedingly disagreeable to the olfactory sensation. There was a continual hum of mosquito[e]s, for an instant like a deep bass, but ended in a shrill treble on the cheek or forehead. It is amazing how so small a lance can cause so much pain and annoyance. Then there was the graiting chirup, chirup of crickets, the distant hoot of an owl in the woods, fireflies[245] dancing in and out through the windows without glass, and at intervals amid all these nocturnal sounds came the bung of a bullfrog from Peter Brillinger's Mill Pond.[246] When our surrounds became so overwhelmingly agai[n]st us and present appearances indicate that things will never come right again, experience teaches that gradually things begin to men. What strikes the ey and ear at first as veritable horrors, begin to be taken as a mat[t]er of couse, and we become at least partially reconcilled to our midnight musicians.

Back Stories of Chapter Nine

Charles J. Brodie

Charles J. Brodie (1834–) is my great-great-grandfather. He married Ellen Spoffard, and their children were Harriet Jane (my great-grandmother), Charles J., George, Mary, William and Mable (1878–?), whom my sisters and I knew and called Aunt Mable. In *History of Toronto and the County of York*, it was stated that he was a member of the Township Council and a Deputy Reeve (Graehem Mercer et al., 1885: 451).

The Gold Medal Winning Farm

In 1890, the Department of Agriculture awarded Cragieburn Farm a gold medal, the only farm that year to be so awarded. It is clear from the words of the committee that they appreciated the scientific nature with

243. AB "sanatary."

244. AB "efficiency."

245. AB "fireflys."

246. Peter Brillinger (1788–1865) was born in Pennsylvania and owned lot 10, concession five. The pond, almost a lake, is still there by the northwest corner of where Stouffville road and the old 5th Concession used to meet. The waterfalls my parents, sisters and I could always see when we went to the farm. On the rare occasion when I drive to the Stouffville area, I look for the waterfalls as a reminder of those days..

which he approached farming.

It is interesting to me personally that two aspects of the farm first commented on were the private road that went down the centre of the farm, and the newly planted Norway spruces. Having travelled that road many times with my grandfather in his old Mercury, and having entered the farm through the evergreen tunnel of the mature spruce, they are two aspects of the farm that never failed to charm the young lad that I was.

Craigieburn Farm, (Annual Report of the Minister of Agriculture and Food, Ontario, 45th Annual Report, Sessional Papers, volume 23, part 2, pp. 27–30):

This splendidly managed farm is lot 2 con. 5, Township of Whitchurch, and is owned by Mr. C. J. Brodie. It comprises 100 acres, of which six acres on the north-east corner is a hardwood bush. A private road runs up the centre of the farm, opening into the wood lot at the rear. This is one of the best made and kept roads that we have seen on any farm that has at any time come under our inspection. The fences on either side of this road are what is known as straight rail, that is, a strong cedar post is set at the end of each panel of an upright piece is fastened to it with wire; the ends of the rails here join. These fences were beautiful, made as straight as a surveyor's line. Good and well-made gates open to into a row of fields on either side....

What took our attention amongst other things when walking through the farm, was that not a stone, stick or rubbish of any sort, was to be seen either on private road, field or fence corner; what stones had been used were drawn into a pile at the back of the farm adjoining the wood lot. But what we did see were fields absolutely clean and free from thistles and all other noxious weeds, good and even crops, a twelve acre field of roots which gave the unmistakeable evidence that Mr. Brodie has a decided liking for going the nearest way across a field, and here and there a fine shade tree.

Considerable has been done in planting Norway spruce, which in a few years will be both ornamental and serve a good purpose as a wind break....

The barn was substantial, 100 feet by 54, built on top of a stone wall that was 12 feet high. It contained horse stables, cattle stables (for 12 head—a stock bull descended from an imported stud bull, a yearling bull, six cows and four calves), and a root cellar.

[In the last part of the report, we see that my great, great grandfather's willingness to use science to improve his farming was a striking part of the committee's appreciation for the man.]

Having at our second inspection of this farm, on the 15th of

September, again gone thoroughly over it with the view of more carefully reporting than the notes of our first visit enable us to do, we were kindly invited to remain over night and then we found out that Mrs Brodie in her department was quite as good a manager as Mr. Brodie was in his. A very pleasant evening we spent in that comfortable farmhouse. We there fully realized that they and their family were doing their share towards placing agriculture on a higher level and giving to farmers a better status. Mr. Brodie is not one of those who think he knows all that is to be learned about farming, or who sneers at those who believe that the light of science is doing much to develop the hidden mysteries of our profession.

Two of his sons have been amongst the brightest students at our Agricultural College. One of them taking the highest honours being the gold medalist of 1889.

Men like Mr. Brodie do much to ennoble our calling, they show that science and practice reflect light on each other, the more to be desired is this for there is no pursuit in which habit is so inveterate or unyielding as amongst those who cultivate the soil (1891: 29).

William Brodie

Uncle Alex's mention of childhood discussions concerning mud wasps is particularly interesting when you consider that his younger brother William Brodie (1831–1909), although earning his money as a dentist, became a well-known entomologist (person who studies insects), founded the Toronto Entomology society in 1877, and some years later became the first provincial entomologist. His specialty was galls and gall insects, such as gall wasps that create those bumps in plants that include an incubating insect larvae.

The Brodie Club, "a group of serious and knowledgeable naturalists who enjoy lively discussion, penetrating questions and good fellowship," was named in his honour after his death, and continues to this day (the brodieclub.eeb.utoronto.ca).

George Mortimer

George Mortimer (1784–1844) was born in London, and was ordained as an Anglican minister in 1811. He came to Upper Canada in 1832, and was made the first rector of the Holy Trinity Church in Thornhill. He had six children, three daughters (of whom one was given the land that the Brodies bought) and three sons. Early becoming well-connected with the Anglican hierarchy and the well-to-do, he became a prominent figure in Upper Canada.

Francis Grose

Francis Grose (c. 1731–1791), sometimes known as Captain Grose and Captain O'Grose, was an antiquarian, and wrote several books on the antiquities of Britain, including two volumes of *Antiquities of Scotland*. Robert Burns wrote a satirical poem about him, called "On Captain Grose's Peregrinations through Scotland."

Macadamizing Roads or Stone Roads

The process of macadamizing roads, named after its inventor Scottish engineer/road-builder John Loudon McAdam (1756–1836), involved placing and compacting on roads several layers of crushed stone. The process was invented in 1820, and first was used in North America in 1822 in a 16 km stretch of road in Maryland. The Upper Canada Legislature voted to have portions of Yonge Street macadamized in 1833. When tar was added to the process it became known as "tarmac" (i.e., Tar MacAdam).

Chapter Ten
The People of the Area

I will now endeavour to say something of the people we had come among to make our home. What really was their[247] opinion of us, or about us, could only be gleaned from their manner and questions. For a year at least we were isolated from church services of any kind. The Revd William Jenkins a Secession[248] Minister preached every third Sabbath in an old school house nearby [86] his own home a few miles away. The Ranter Methodists[249] had a little church at [250] Reid's [C]orners four miles away. Under these untoward circumstances my father gathered us all together and we read a chapter apiece, he read a psalm and engaged in prayer. Very often a man and his wife would look in at the door or window when the worship was going on, and steal away again. But by the time one year had come and gone they became reconciled, that we had not come from the Moon or the Fugee[251] Islands. These people were Canadians, or rather American Canadians pure and simple. They did not harm, they wished us no harm, but they were shockingly deficient in manners not to speak of etiquette.

The population of the county of York at least in our neighborhood was largely composed of Dutch from Pen[n]sylvania and the Mohawk Valley, State of New York. There was a more or less sprinkling of English, mostly from the northern Counties. The ubiquitous Scot and Irishman more or less represented according to locality though few Scotch were settled very near to us in 1835. There were[252] also a few thorough bred Yankees from down east, with the nasal twang strongly developed. I can only remember a few not over a dozen who claimed to be U. E. Loyalists. Several Americans who denied having any affinity to Dutch, down Easter or any other American ilk. They considered themselves higher in the gamut of mental calibre than Dutch or Down Easter and ig[n]ored the name of Yankee with indignity. It is necessary for the sequel of my story to dilute[253] briefly on the

---

247. AB "there."

248. This was a branch of the Presbyterian church that separated from the main branch. For the story of Rev. William Jenkins, see Back Stories in this chapter.

249. The Primitive Methodists built a church there early in the 1830s. They were known as "Ranters" because of the camp meeting style of their services.

250. AB "Reads."

251. It is the Fiji Islands that are meant here. In the early 19th century they were referred to sometimes as the Fugee Islands.

252. AB "was."

253. I think that he meant to write "digress" here.

peculiarlities[254] or id[i]osyncrasys of the people compositing[255] this mixed population.

The Pennsylvania and New York "Dutch"

The Dutch from Pen[n]sylvania and the Mohawk Valley were the first settlers in the Townships of York, Vaug[ha]n, Markham, **[87]** Whitchurch south of the Ridges. North of the Ridges around Newmarket was known in the early days as the Quaker Settlement, sometimes as Upper Settlement. The Quakers were not Dutch, but they came from Pen[n]sylvania, and undoubtedly descendents of the Quakers who settled under William Penn's colonization scheme. They were good people and thrifty settlers had beautiful farms in 1835.

The Pen[n]sylvania Dutch were a kind peaceable[256] people. Better neighbors could not be as long as they were treated honestly and faithfully. An untruthful man had no place with them. If any one of them found a man tricky[257] in dealing he immediately became ostracized by the whole Dutch fraternity. In religion they were either Tunkers or Men[n]onites. Just as to the tenets of the Tunkers I am not fully acqua[i]nted.[258] Think they originated in Germany and might be one of the northern Provinces of Holland, about the time of the Reformation and taook advantage of Penn's schem[e] along with the Men[259][n]onites. They held a feast once a year generally in June. With them it was a religious festival but any could partake of their hospitality if they choose. Of course there was preaching and prayer, and praise all in the Dutch[260] language. The men wash others['] feet, so do the women. I never witnessed a baptism but have been told they baptise by immersion. Dip three times, first in the name of the Father, second in the name of the Son. Third in the name of the Holy Spirit. Sixty to seventy years ago many of them wore long full beards. Wore about the same costume as the Men[n]onites. During the thirties and forties and perhaps up to the present time they met in another's houses for worship, in a kind of rotation. It was understood that the member in whose house the meeting was held entertained the worship[p]ers, at least **[88]** those who chose to remain, with a substantial repast, and their horses fed.

In so far as I have learned the Mennonites are the followers of Men[n]o Simon who during the middle of the sixteenth century, when Holland was

254. AB "peculiarliarities."

255. I think that he meant to write "composing" here.

256. AB "peacible."

257. AB "trickey."

258. See Back Stories in this chapter.

259. AB "Menonites" here and elsewhere.

260. That is, "Deutsch" or German.

much agitated about the Reformation, founded a religious sect known as Mennonites in the Dutch Province of Friesland. In due time he had many followers. He taught them that infant baptism was unscriptural, swearing, taking an oath in a court of law, to go to Law, to go]to] war, to cherish revenge, to hold an office under a government, to be ostenta[t]ious in dress were[261] sinful. He taught a very high standard of Christian character. He believed in an ordained Ministry but no pay. Men[n]o must have been a powerful man for after the lapse of three and a half centuries forced to move from one country to another, suffer many trials and persecutions, the Mennonite Church in all its branches retain the fundamental principles laid down and taught by Men[n]o to this day.

They had to leave Holland on account of Military service. A number came to America and settled in Pennsylvania under Penn's scheme, but the great majority moved to the northern part of Prussia. Military service again compelled them to seek another home. They were severely treated by the Prussian Government. Catherine the 2nd of Russia[262] offered them an asylum in a newly acquired territory along the Black Sea, with immunity from military service. The Mennonites accepted this offer and moved to this territory. Here they remained until 1870, they enjoyed all the privileges desired for one hundred years. They became wealthy, generally engaged in agricultural pursuits, although many became prominent as merchants and [89] manufacturers. But trouble came again. The Russian Government took no notice of the bargain with Catherine and confirmed by Paul the 2nd.[263] But again enforced military service, hence the emigration to Manitoba and the Northwest Territories. Do not know just what special privileges our Government has confer[r]ed on them.

In the Counties of York and Waterloo, both Tunkers and Mennonites exempt from military service by paying a light tax away back in the thirties, but I do not think it very closely exacted. It was alleged by certain Wags[264] that certain young Dutchmen were so derelict to the orthodox Dutch coat, which was peculiar in shape, very much like pum[p]kin seed, small end down. A small straight standing up collar, and the useless though stereotyped two buttons on the back wholly disregarded as to have the two buttons on the back fully exposed to view, and tail not so much circumscribed. But when the training day came around exit the two buttons on the back and by some mysterious cantrip the collar was transformed into the orthodox again. In 1835 and for many years after that date, the costume was the insignia of who were Tunkers, Mennonites, or Quakers, being members in

---

261. AB "was."

262. Also known as Catherine the Great (1729–1796).

263. The son of Catherine the Great, Paul was Tsar for five years (1754–1801).

264. A somewhat archaic use of the term "wag" is referring to someone who jokes about something or someone, often a public figure.

full communion with their respective churches, this did not apply exclusively to young men and young women, members of so called families not members in full communion.

The Mohawk Dutch were descendents of the Hollanders that pioneered [New] York state. Although the Pennsylvania Mennonite and Tunker were originally of the same stock as the Mohawk, yet they were different as a people. Religious customs and perhaps coming from a Province of Holland a distance from the scene of Menno's teaching. The language and general deportment of the [90] Mohawks were quite the opposite of each other, had nothing in common with the staid tacit Pennsylvanians. Few of them were with Mennonites or Tunkers. They looked upon the dress and manners of the Mennonites and Tunkers as great folly, and away behind the times. They seemed to assimilate more with other nationalities than the Pennsylvanians. But to an unprejudiced observer might have been in a doubt whether they were any improvement as citizens to the unpretending Mennonite and Tunker.

These different types of American people had been influenced to leave their native states, by the excellent free grant land across the lines, (York) Toronto was founded in 1794 by Governor Simcoe. Between that date and 1812 many American people had settled within a radius of twenty miles north, east, and west of Toronto, and still kept coming a family now and then up to 1835. It must be remembered that, from 1783 to 1812 only 29 years had elapsed since Great Britain recognized the independence of her revolted Colonies. So the change from the new Republic to the old flag was of minor importance when temporal advantages were paramount.

These Dutch settlers were thorough woodsmen. Had handled the axe and handspike[265] from boyhood. In all things pertain[in]g to the clearing of land they were experts. They were experienced in all concomitants of pioneer life, from the building [of] the primitive shanty, to the great hewed log barn. Though of different material yet its prototype is quite common in Holland today in some of the northern Provinces. They were strong men, and strong women and the enterprize they engaged in, and their success proved they were possessed of indomitable perseverance. They endured all the troubles [91] and turmoil consequent to making a home in the forest primeval.

Although professing no scientific knowledge of geology they knew good land, though ignorant of zoology in a scientific sense they knew the way of the denizens of the forest, their habits and resorts. They knew the[266] way of birds, from the humming bird to the bald eagle, knowing little of

265. A handspike is a metal or, earlier, wooden bar used typically as a kind of lever. It was used in ways similar to a crowbar, only it is in the shape of a spike, with a pointed and a blunt end.

266. AB "they."

ornithology, only by experience. They knew all about snakes native to the country from the little garter to the rat[t]ler, perhaps having never heard of op[h]iology[267] since they were born. They knew some[e]thing of medicinal plants, wild and tame, and the women were no novices in administering to the sick. Medical men and trained nurses of today would no doubt condemn some of their antidotes as bordering on the mystic. Nevertheless mean and women grew up from such nursing, and hygiene as assisted materially in making the County of York one of the wealthiest in the Province.

These men knew the best locations for grist mills[268] and sawmills. From the founding of York up to 1820 they had the choice of several Townships and already had clearly proved their judgement in the value of the selections they had made. Many of them had four hundred acres on block for simply clearing a few acres. In 1835 many of them had large clearances, or at least one hundred acres being the homestead. Had comfortable log houses, and here and there a new frame barn and house were being built. In fact large frame bank barns[269] they were called were to be seen among the wealthy Dutch farmers, taking the place of the once common log one, of the same style of architecture two mows[270] and the threshing floor between. Log barns like many other conveniences of old Canadian days have passed away in old **[92]** Ontario never to return. One of the first investments after a small clearance had been made was to plant an orchard. So in 1835 apples, cherries, plums, and the smaller fruits were abundant among the first settlers.

Whether water was scarce in Pennsylvania and New York I never heard them say, but they placed great value on a farm with a creek running through it, of which there were many south of the ridges in early days of settlement, where I have caught large trout in the thirties now about dried up except perhaps a muddy gurgling just in spring and fall. It was no uncommon thing to find sixty five to seventy years ago to find the buildings near a spring creek away at the rear end of the farm.[271] Quite a number of the settlers in 1835 had wells to supply the house, but to pump water to supply stock was in their estimation a [kind] of supererogation, and windmills were away in the future.

The settlers from the British islands were much beholden to the Amer-

---

267. From the Greek word for snake, meaning the study of snakes.

268. Grist mills are those in which grain (e.g., corn and wheat) is ground into flour.

269. Bank barns are accessible from two different levels, often being built on the side of a hill or bank. Ramps could be built to artificially create the same effect.

270. A mow is a place in the barn where grain, straw or hay is stored (i.e., something that has been mowed).

271. On the Brodie farm, there was a stream at the back of the land, where a pond for fishing had been created. I fished there, and helped, in a small way, my grandfather maintain the pond. There was a pump not far from the barn, and a short walk away from the house.

ican Canadian in clearing land, building log houses, making sleighs, jumpers, splitting rails, making maple sugar, using the grain cradle, and many other jobs peculiar to roughing it in the woods. On the other hand the Canadian pioneer was greatly indebted to the old countryman[272] in the practical work on the farm, care and breeding of stock, introducing improved farming implements. In fact horses, cattle, sheep and swine of improved breeds were almost exclusively imported by old countrymen. They likewise in a few years brought about a better system of cropping. After the stumps were somewhat gotten rid of[273] the early pioneers were as a rule far from being up to date farmers. They were neither practical nor theoretical. Their implements were wholly inadequate, as the land became firmer by tillage. They were no ploughmen neither were they in the least discouraged by knowing the fact. [93]

Their[274] ploughs were primeval in every sense of the word. I might try to describe it but to convey a correct mental picture of the mechanism would be impossible. The picture of the Egyptian plough, in the days of the Pharaohs as we see it in old pictures would hardly be a prototype on its work. The handles were almost perpendicular, the beam short and straight with means, I may say no means sufficient to regulate width and depth o[f] furrow. A wooden mold board[275] was made with little regard to shape in lifting and turning the furrow to any angle. The share[276] was little more than an iron pike nailed on to a wooden sole and in some indescribable manner was attached to the coulter.[277] The coulter in some mysterious manner was fixed to the beam to remain there until its days were done. There was no such thing as sharpening coulter or share, the implement was so near the oxen that the ploug[h]man could easily reach them with a gad,[278] which he held in his right hand letting it trail behind when not using it. It was left handed, and to the eye of a Scotch or Englishman was unique in the extreme.[279] A few of the Dutch families in our neighborhood stuck to this miserable caricature for a plough as long as they possible could.

272. The "Old Country" referred to here is Britain.

273. AB "off."

274. AB "there."

275. The moldboard is the curved piece, usually made of metal, that turns the earth aside from the furrow.

276. The ploughshare or share is the cutting or leading edge of the moldboard.

277. The coulter is the ground breaking spike in front of the ploughshare.

278. A gad was a sharp stick used in driving oxen.

279. This means that the American way of driving oxen or horses was to stand on the left (just as the driver's side in a car is on the left) and that the British way of doing so was on the right (just as in Britain the driver sits on the righthand side).

Among those were the Brilli[n]gers[280] just across the concession from our house. They claimed they had an important advantage over our long plough, and other improved ploug[h]s being introduced, that in ploughing among stumps it was impossible for a root to get in between the share and coulter, which often caused a good deal of trouble before the roots were rotten. Also that they required no headband. Still they made out to till the land in a kind of way and raised faire crops the virgin fertility not being exhausted. A blacksmith from Aberdeenshire, John Finnie, came to the country in 1835 and **[94]** manufactured the long swing Scotch plough after the pat[t]ern of the celebrated Mitchell ploughs of Peterhead. This plough was as great a curiosity to the Dutch people as the medieval implement was to the old countryman but the Canadian soon learned the benefit of the improved plough still the exclusively old fashioned Dutchmen would have theirs left handed.[281]

The Scots vs. the Oxen

My father did his best to log up a half cleared patch to get a little fall wheat in for next year[']s bread. I have almost forgot to tell that our farm was lot 2 Concession 5, Township of Whitchurch. My father bought a yoke of oxen from a Dutchman, <u>Darby</u> and <u>Bright</u>, with yoke and chain for seventy dollars, and three year old heifer coming in with two little pigs thrown in for sixteen dollars. The oxen were reputed one of the best teams in the neighborhood. So they were when our nearest neighbor Philip Gower drove them, they were all that could be desired. When he went away they refused to obey. Still with great perseverance and much discouragement we got the logs together and burned. It seemed to be a matter of fun to the Canadians to observe our first attempts at logging. One day an old man came past, stood for an instant or two with an amused ghost of a smile on his fact, then laughed outright, and said "I think I can make them oxen draw that log." No doubt he was amused at my father[']s vain efforts to get the log in over to the heap. My father said, "I wish you would," and handed him the gad. He laid down a skid, put a roll on the chain, rolled the log on the skid and by geeing[282] and hawing from one side to another changing the skid or skids, and threatening in the most clas[s]ic Billingsgate to anni-

---

280. See footnote in Chapter 9.

281. For a picture of a left-handed plow see, see Image 0057, between pages 36–7, in Reaman, George Elmore, 1971, *A History of Vaughan Township*, Vaughan Township Historical Society, printed by University of Toronto Press (www.ourroots.ca/e/toc.aspx?id=8222).

282. Geeing and hawing refers to commands given to draught animals. The command "gee" means to go away from the driver (to the right in the American way and to the left in the British way). The command "haw" means to come towards the driver (to the left in the American way and to the right in the British way).

hilate them if they did not pull, he succeeded in getting the log to the side of the heap.

But the oxen knew they had no master. When attempt was made to plough with them they refused to put straight ahead. They ran away with the plough, they would gee around onto what was already[283] ploughed then haw around on the land. They did everything but the right thing. [95] It was very provoking. My mother and Betty came to condole. Betty suggested that <u>maybe</u> the beasts did not understand Scotch. But the man was angered beyond endurance,[284] beyond the limit of suffering. It was evident a crisis was at hand. He called to me to run to the house and tell Sandy[285] to come down as fast as he could. Sandy came and was instructed to keep the plough in with a good heavy furrow as well as he could. What had once been the handle of a hickory broom by some means was at hand. The handle was tough and stout, the knot on the end where the splints had been, thick and sound. He rolled up his shirt sleeves to his shoulders and grasped the stick in both hands, while the family stood around looking at each other, and at every move in the drama that was to be immediately acted with intense interest. The blood of many ancestors was coursing in his veins. It was a fight to the finish. The oxen were placed in position in the plough and told to get up, they attempted to gee around when hickory stick flashed through the air like a meteor and came down on Darby's back. There was a thud and something like a puff of smoke and a tuft of hair floated away on the summer breeze. His belly came near to the ground and he wagged his tail, indicative[286] of a new experience in ploughing. "I'll make you understand me." He said, and he did. Once or twice they tried to run away, but a stroke from the hickory between t he nose and the eyes that caused the blood to drop freely from their nostrils put a stop to that prank. In less than half an hour their tongues were lolling out of their mouths but there was no respect until night. After this experience they were the most obedient oxen anyone could wish [to have]. There is no use to talk about dumb brutes and that thing called instinct. These oxen in three hours' time understood the Aberdeen doric just as well as if they had be reared in the House o' Buchan.

Back Stories of Chapter Ten

Rev. William Jenkins

Rev. William Jenkins (1779–1843) was raised in the relatively radical tradition of the Free Church in Scotland. His early work in North America was as a missionary to the Oneida in New York. By 1817 (perhaps a

283. AB "a kind."

284. AB "indurance."

285. This was Sandy Morrison.

286. AB "indacative."

year earlier) he came to Upper Canada, and acted as an itinerant preacher to congregations in Scarborough and Richmond Hill, not far south of the Brodie farm. Because of his radical religious background, he seems not to been allowed to have steady work in a stable congregation. That is why when the Brodies first knew about him, he was preaching out of his house (my.tbay.tel/bmartin/Jenkins.htm).

The Dunkers

The Dunkers (also Tunkers, Tunkards and Dunkards) began as a religious sect in 1708 in what is now the Schwarzenau region of mid-western Germany. They opposed what they believed to be the corrupt religion of the established and recognized churches of Catholicism, Lutheranism and Reformed Lutheranism. State and religious opposition caused many to leave for the United States for Pennsylvania under the colonial enterprise proposed by William Penn (1644–1718), a Quaker dedicated to religious freedom who was given a large piece of land (Pennsylvania and Delaware) by Charles II of Britain to pay off a debt. The years 1719–33 saw several groups move to Pennsylvania. Dunkers' beliefs and practices included full immersion baptism (hence the name Dunkers), pacificism, anti-slavery, abstinence from alcohol, and simplicity and modesty in clothing and in their churches. The name of the group later was changed from Dunkers to Brethren in Christ.

The Mennonites

Mennonites are a Christian religious sect named after Menno Simons (1496–1561) of Friesland (a province in the northwest of the Netherlands), a Roman Catholic priest who challenged the church in which he was raised. Like the Dunkers, the radical beliefs of the Mennonites included a similar dedication to pacificism, adult baptism, being a church member by choice rather than by order of the state, an emphasis on community and a lack of rigid religious hierarchy. Along with similar new religious sects of the time, it was persecuted but spread in the 16th and 17th centuries to a number of different areas of Western Europe, including Germany, Austria and Switzerland. When William Penn broadcast his idea of settlement in America, a good number of Mennonites joined.

Uncle Alex's niece, Harriet Jane, daughter of his youngest brother Charles, married a Mennonite, the handsome Abram Steckley, my great-grandfather.

Scottish Emigrants to Canada

In the year that the Brodies sailed on the Alert there were 7,108 Irish, 3,067 English and 2,127 Scottish emigrants travelling to Quebec. For every year from 1829 to 1853 that numerical order was followed (Campey 2005:

163). For the years 1831–55, the main Scottish ports were Glasgow, Greenock and Aberdeen, with 28,238, 18,008, and 10,409 emigrants respectively. Unfortunately, the table that contains these figures includes Peterhead as one of "Misc[ellaneous]. Small Ports," which had a total altogether of 5,459 (Campey 2005: 158).

Uncle Alex did not mention the presence of presence of Scots settlers in the immediate area. In Campey (2002: 132) there is a map of Scottish settlement by 1851 (Figure 5: Concentration of Scottish-born settlers in Western Upper Canada, 1851). In this map are indicated the highly concentrated and moderately concentrated "Scottish clusters." Included in the former are groups found immediately east and west of Lake Simcoe, two in Middlesex County and one large one immediately east of that county, a very short distance from where Uncle Alex would settle with his family by the 1870s. York County had neither highly concentrated or even moderately concentrated clusters anywhere. The Brodies would be different from their settler neighbours in country of origin.

Chapter Eleven[287]
Making Maple Syrup and Rebellion in Upper Canada

Maple Syrup Making in the Upper Canada Bush

During the winter of 1836 we chopped ten acres and got it ready for wheat in the fall. We were greatly obliged to our neighbor Philip Gower for instructions in falling trees to the best advantage for logging. Of this old pioneer I will have to revert again. In the meantime he came to make sugar in our bush on shares. He found the kettle, made the spiles[288] and tapped the trees of course, the troughs were in the bush and got one half of the sugar and molasses. The gathering of the sap, getting wood and other work was a kind of Co. Partnership affair. There was old Philip, young Philip, my father, Geordie, and Jamie, I being deemed unworthy of being partner in the Co. Whatever Jamie did, or did not do, or what was transgression of the Company's rules or regulations was never very well defined. At all events Philip said he was no good, he ate more bellygut[289] and drank more syrup than his work was worth. Jamie bunged,[290] huffed came home in a very unpleasant state of mind declaring he would never go back to the camp again as long as Philip was there.

The result of this estrangement between Philip and Jamie was that Jamie and I with the help of our mother, who gave us every dish that could be spared that would hold sap was utilized. We tapped perhaps twenty five trees nearest the house in the chopping. Boiled the sap in the house fire, the pots suspended from the crane or sgey[291] we called it. The sap collected from these dishes was wholly immune from all foreign matter. We did not boil the sap down to very thick syrup before straining, allowed it to settle a night before sugaring off. Philip was a little uneasy as to the manner [in which] he had spoken to Jamie and every time my father went to the bush he laughingly inquired how Jamie was getting on sugar making. Philip had no doubt Jamie's sugar making would be a total failure. Well we sugared off trying it the way we had seen Philip do. We had just hit **[97]** the right test when to take it off and this on first sugaring off proved to be a signal success. The sugar was as white as the driven snow. My father had been dubious of Jamie's knowledge of the proper time to take of[f] the kettle and was greatly astonished to see the beautiful white sugar. Nor was the whiteness all its excellence, the granulations were complete and the rich

---

287. This is Chapter 10 in the original, the last numbered chapter created by Uncle Alex.

288. Spiles are the hollow wooden or metal pegs hammered into the maple tree. The sap flows through them and into the pail hanging from the spile.

289. Bellygut is a Scots term for glutton, but I am not sure of the exact meaning here.

290. Bunged is a Scots expression for taking offence or becoming sulky.

291. The second letter here is difficult to determine.

taste was superlative beyond any of the maple sugar we had tasted before. Father took a sample back to the woods to let Philip see Jamie's success. "Zounds", he said, "What has the boy put into it?" The boy put nothing into it but he kept everything out, nothing but pure sap was boiled, care being taken that light ashes or any other dust should not get into the pots during the boiling down process. Such sugar was never seen in the neighborhood before and many were[292] the conjectures as to some mystic cantrip that Jamie had exercised to produce it. He continued to make the same quality of sugar during the seasons. I may just mention here that a sample of this sugar was sent home to Peterhead and was the sensation of the Town for sometime, and many congratulations came back as to our good fortune in getting such excellent sugar without paying money for it.

Towards the end of 1837 we had got along as far as bought a span[293] of colts, they had ploughed a little in the fall but had never been hitched to wagon or sleigh. They were to be broken in when sleighing came. We had been longing for the luxury of the old settlers in their comfortable sleighs, sleek horses and merry tinkling bells. While we had to go to the mill away across the ridges to Bogart's mill[294] nearly ten miles, or Cook's mill[295] in Vaugh[a]n just as far, these being the only two mills that had smut machines and made good flour, for many miles around. It was rather aggravating to see the horse sleighs drive past us so often in the road. It took one whole day from early morning until night **[98]** to go and come and when the mills were busy in winter, it was often a week to wait for the grist and then had to go back a second time was a great trouble.

The Rebellion of 1837

There was quite an [ag]itation in the County during 1837. Politics had become almost a mania. Without dismissing the various causes that led[296] up to the rebellion and its results, I will say nothing further than necessary to the subsequent events of my story. Those who have not experienced the mental strain on the people consequent in living in a country or community during a civil war cannot realize its effects. Neighbors who have lived in most social companionship previous to hostilities, yea, even by ties more

---

292. AB "was."

293. A "span" refers to a pair of draught animals such as horses or oxen who are hitched together, side by side.

294. In 1805 John Bogart built a saw mill, then a grist mill on the Holland River the next year in what is now called Bogarttown, a community now generally included as part of Newmarket ("A Brief History of the Town of Newmarket", www.newmarket.ca/Thingstodo/Document/History%20-%20Terry%20Carter%20Compilation.pdf).

295. It would be located on the West Don River, and, judging from the current presence of a Cook's Mill Crescent in the area, north of Rutherford Road and west of Bathurst.

296. AB "lead."

sacred than personal esteem, become bitter enemies. It might be an ethical question just what causes that innate bias towards one side, more than another, in a <u>ca[s]us belli</u>.[297] We might assume ambition, aggrandizement, patriotism, and love of self and other sinister motives. But whatever might be the motives for differences of opinion in choosing between rebellion and adhering to the powers that be, must be looked for generally in the household sentiments. Still it is difficult to reconcile how men living in peace and tranquility could possible [en]gender such animosity towards each other as to become unmitigated enemies.[298] We have heard and read of unalloyed generosity of men on different sides in war towards each other. But the history of civil wars tell the story that there is still a trait of the <u>savage</u> in our nature notwithstanding our boasted civilization[299] and Christianity.

A state of society somewhat as I have described more or less pervaded the people in the County of York, especially in the Townships of Markham, York, Vaughan, Whitchurch, and Uxbridge, towards the end of 1837. Of course for a few years previous to this date there had been much political rancour, East York being the constituency W. L. Mackenzie **[99]** was elected for five times and as many times expelled.[300] The House of Assembly, refusing to issue a writ of election for three years. In consequence of these unconstitutional measures Mackenzie had many friends and sympathizers in the Townships immediately north of Toronto.

Notwithstanding the great pecuniary benefits the American settlers received in crossing the lines to Canada which a Paternal Government had given them for simply clearing a few acres, the choice of the best land and locations in the County, their sympathy was largely with the Mackenzie party. By the year 1835 they had all or nearly all become British subjects. Many of them had fought on the British side in 1812 and 13 and proved themselves[301] no poltroons.[302] The majority of them hesitated before casting aside the axe and handspike and shouldering a musket. But the feeling was hostile to the Government at Toronto, which they regarded as nothing better than a petty Oligarchy. In short, Government by the Family Compact.[303] This hostile feeling was not so much against the home government, in so far as the crown had dealt with the Settlers, but they believed the Colonial Office was imposed upon by false statements through the influ-

---

297. This is Latin, literally meaning "a case for war." It refers to the justifications or causes of a particular war.

298. AB "enimies."

299. AB "civilazation."

300. See Back Stories in this chapter (William Lyon Mackenzie).

301. AB "themselelves."

302. AB "paltroons."

303. See Back Stories in this chapter.

ence of the family compact, and the supinesses[304] of Sir Francis Bond Head and former Governors all being duped as to the vital cause of disaffection. Bond Head was either unwilling or dilatory in investigating the grievances complained of, hence the home Government [was] remiss in hearing the true state of affairs as revealed to the Colonial Secretary by Mackenzie who was sent to England as a delegate from the reform party to unmask the maladministration of the family compact, not only in matters of state, wholly unconstitutional, but all emolument arising or flowing from the affairs of government was sucked into the greedy Maw of the family compact. This indifference to people's appeal by the Colonial department aroused the indignation **[100]** of the liberal party causing much ill feeling towards the Government and Council.

A young Englishman from Yorkshire with the very prosaic name of William Smith,[305] had settled about the same time as my father on an a[d]joining lot. William and my father me first at a logging bee, being new beginners they were considered no good in a race, consequently were not chose until the last. The teamster, a good natured Dutchman, when he saw they were willing and strong, gave them a few lesson, and as it happened opportunely the other two men in the company were jocund[306] sons of Erin who had only been in the country one year previous and knew how to sympathize with strangers. Four rollers[307] and a teamster composed a logging compa[n]y. It was soon noticed that the old sods as they were called had a fair proportion of bone and mu[s]cle in their corporeity. They could give and take a joke, still were not likely to be imposed upon. Nemo me impune lacessit.[308] Some kind of magnetic influence attracted William and my father at this first logging bee to become fast friends until death severed the bond.

On the seventh of December 1837 memorable in Canadian history as the date of the utter defeat and discomfiture of the insurgent party at Gallows Hill[309] about four miles north of Toronto. Memorable to the descendents of those who lost their lives in that ill fated uprising. Especially[310] memorable to us as a family as the reader of this nar[r]ative will soon learn.

---

304. This can be translated as "acts of apathy." Supineness can be translated as apathy or passivity. I don't believe this noun has a plural.

305. William Smith (1813–1882).

306. Cheerful or lighthearted.

307. AB "rollars."

308. AB "lecenit." This was the Latin motto of the Stuart royal line, and of three Scottish regiments in the British army. It means "No one cuts (i.e., attacks) me with impunity." The Family Compact used it as their Latin motto.

309. See Back Stories in this chapter (Gallows Hill).

310. AB "sepecially."

The Memoirs of Alexander Brodie

On this date William Smith came to assist my father to make a jumper,[311] preparatory to having a sleigh ride on Christmas day. It was an intensely cold day though not much snow on the ground. The conversation during the day apart from the work on the jumper, was, naturally about the expected battle, and its consequences. My father and mother never doubted the ultimate result be the complete overthrow of the Mackenzie party. William though a true Briton was rather in favour of the Mackenzie party, as they were against the [101] hated family compact. We knew several men who had gone down to join Mackenzie's army, and a good deal of conjecture and jests were made during the day as to who would stand fire, and who would run away. It was rumoured around that a certain young man got a breastplate made before he went down to the battle. And old Englishman going into the house one morning saw the queer looking thing, and inquired what it was for. The young man said, taking it in his hand, "I will put this under my vest, and defy any tory bullet to hurt me." Old England smiled[312] significantly, gave a few puffs from his pipe, and suggested another place to up it where it [might serve] a better purpose. Sure enough the young fellow came home with a bullet in the very place suggested by the old Englishman.

Back Stories of Chapter Eleven

The Family Compact

The Family Compact refers to a group of men who had a great deal of power in Upper Canada from the 1810s to the 1840s in their dominance of the legal profession, land ownership, financial institutions, and political positions. They belonged to the first wave of Loyalists, coming either directly from Britain or from the United States prior to the War of 1812. They generally held distrusted the "later Loyalists," and tried to prevent them from being able to swear allegiance, thus blocking them from land grants. Without owning land you could neither vote nor hold public office. Politically the members of the Family Compact were Tories or conservatives. In 1839 John George Lambton, Earl of Durham, and Governor-General of British North America issued his Report on the Affairs of British North America, which included a condemnation of the Family Compact, and pushed for some of the reforms that the opposition parties had fought for.

The Family Compact was not strictly family-based, but family was involved. Five of its members were linked through marriage. Solicitor General and then Attorney General and lawyer of the Bank of Upper Canada Henry John Boulton and Levius Sherwood, who was the speaker of the

---

311. I can't tell from this passage whether the "jumper" is a part of the sleigh (a term I can't find), or a kind of sleigh.

312. AB "smiled."

Legislative Council and was judge in the Court of the King's Bench both were married to sisters of Judge Jonas Jones. Boulton's father was G. Darcy Boulton, who was the Auditor General of Upper Canada, and brother-in-law of John Beverley Robinson.

The political structure of Upper Canada had three main bodies: the Executive Council and Legislative Council, which were appointed and were initially meant to have separate membership (though that was not the case in practice), and the elected Legislative Assembly, which had a lot less power. The Family Compact dominated the upper two bodies and tried to control through a variety of means legitimate and illegitimate the Legislative Assembly. Their official job was to "advise" the Lieutenant-Governor regarding policy.

Sir John Beverley Robinson, appointed as the first Baronet (hence the "Sir") of Toronto, who after first becoming Solicitor General and then Attorney General became the Chief Justice of Upper Canada for 34 years beginning in 1829, was generally thought of as the leader of the Family Compact.

William Allan held positions in both councils, was President of the Toronto and Lake Huron Railroad, Governor of the British American Fire and Life Assurance Company, and President of the Board of Trade, and President of the Bank of Upper Canada from 1822 to 1835.

Bishop John Strachan was a force for the Church of England or Anglican Church in Upper Canada. He was very sectarian, opposing both the Methodist and Presbyterian churches. This can be seen in his desire to have education controlled by the Anglican Church, and by his arguing that the money from the clergy reserves be given only to that church. The clergy reserves were blocks of land—one-seventh of all surveyed land in Upper Canada—that were set aside for supporting churches. This amounted to some 2,395,687 acres of land. Strachan was a member of the Executive Council from 1815 to 1836, and was appointed the first bishop of Toronto in 1839.

Gallows Hill

Gallows Hill is formed by the drop from the old lake line in Toronto situated roughly along St. Clair Avenue. The place so named is a little south of St. Clair, and a little west of Yonge Street. This was a bit north of Toronto at the time, which ended at Bloor Street. While it is easy to assume that it received its name from the hanging of the rebels, it did not. The story is told that a man committed suicide there by hanging himself, with an unfortunate farmer spotting the sad scene as he drove his carriage north (see Mulvany, Adam and Robinson, 1885, part II, p. 31).

Chapter Twelve
The Indian Raid

The Indian Raid
William [Smith] went home in the evening to do his chores, and we had a roaring fire in the fireplace and stove which we had only to a short time before. Everything was secured for the night. We were anticipating a pleasant evening, in spite of the cold outside. My mother was busy preparing supper, when a few quick hard knocks on the door caused everyone to look towards it. It was "come in" in those days. The door opened just wide enough to allow the honest and pleasant face of William to appear and show itself in the open space, now serious, every line drawn tight, a striking[313] contrast to the usual well pleased smiling face of our good neighbor. He drew a long breath and said with a quaver in his voice, "I've come with bad news to you." My mother stood half way to the table with something in her hand, and said anxiously. "Has anything happened to Mrs. Smith?" Emphatic "no."

"The Indians have entered both Townships, they are coming down scalping, murdering and burning as they come. We are going over to Richard's my brother-in-law's it is on a knoll we can see around and defend ourselves. Hitch your colts into that old ox sled get your wife and family on to it and come with us. Haste man. Let everything go before we are killed ourselves. Quick I [102] may be killed before I get back."

And away he ran at his utmost speed.

William's suggestion of hitching the colts to the ox sled was very kind but wholly impractical. The colts had never been hitched up together in sleigh nor wagon, and moreover there was no tongue in it. For a few minutes it might have been ten, twenty or not over five. I could not describe the scene to convey anything [of] an adequate reality of it from memory seventy one years[314] have passed into history since that eventful evening, and although time has made many changes, and incidents in my life in the past threescore years and ten, yet this one event is still fresh in my memory's page. You will have to imagine more than I can tell. My mother, strong woman as she was mentally and physically, was overwhelmed with grief. In her anguish she cried out:

"Oh why did you take me away to such a terrible place to be murdered with my children, by savages? We were well enough at home. Oh why did we leave our good home in Scotland and come to this dreadful place?"

The three younger children hung around her in terror, clinging to her skirts as if that would afford them protection. The while my father was

---

313. AB "stricking."

314. As the even he was describing took place in 1837, it would be 69 years, not 71.

doing and saying every kind of word and action to pacify her grief. During this time long or short he took little notice of us until he succeeded in getting her fear somewhat abated. But the thought seemed to haunt her:

"Why did we come to this place to be murdered by Indians. Why did we not let well enough alone?"

Experience teaches the fact that as soon as the first paroxysm of fear subsides self preservation takes its place. It is now for dear life to act. The elder boys had been looking to the west, not sure but Indians were hiding among the stumps, perhaps stealing towards our house and it was only a matter of a few minutes or half an hour when a few char[r]ed bones and ashes would mark the place where we once had been. But amid [103] these sad reflections my father called:

"Geordie run over to Peter Brillinger's and learn if they have heard anything of this terrible report and what they are going to do. Jamie you run across to Philip Gower's and find what they are going to do or if they have heard this alarm."

The boys were back about the same time. No one had gone to tell the Brillingers. When told the sorrowful story they were struck dumb in consternation unable to speak, or act when Geordie left them. Jamie came home laughing and said:

"Philip told me to go back as quick as I could and tell your Daddy and Mammy to come down here, bring your guns and pistol, the sword and all the ammunition yo've got. I'll go down to the woods and cut some clubs. Ingins only go four or five in a gang. I aint aferd of a few buck Ingins."

This report though rather doubtful concerning Philip's policy or defence was some consolation besides William's sombrous story, and no time was lost in acting on it. Chests were opened and the most valuable things selected and hastily bundled up blankets wearing apparel, heirlooms, all the bread that was baked, a ham and the Deed to the farm. Everyone had a pack except the baby and we left our home with many misgivings that we would never see it again. When we got to Philip's house he had a good fire blazing in the kitchen and his clubs [were] standing in the corner of the fireplace. They were small trees about one inch in diameter cut out by the roots, the roots of course trimmed off leaving the enlargement intact and a little longer than a staff. A strong man wielding one of these weapons with both hands on an Indian's head would have given him quitus[315] to the happy hunting ground of his tribe instantly.

Philip's house, though not pretentious, was a good large frame house fully up to date in all its concomitants as a Dutch residence, the kitchen and stove room being the principal apartments.[316] Two bedrooms downstairs

---

315. This word is usually used to refer to the discharging of a debt.

316. AB "appartments" here and elsewhere.

[104] and as many beds in the attic as required according to members in family.

Philip's family consisted of his wife, two daughters, and a son known in the neighborhood as young Phil. The oldest daughter, Katy, married Mr. Paul Shell,[317] living close by, Sarah at home a pretty girl of sixteen or eighteen summers best known to the neighbors as Sally.

A man by the name of James Chard had built and started a tavern about a mile east on the Townline. Young Phil was in the habit of frequently going down there in the evenings when he should have been at home. Geordie, Jamie and another young man that called in volunteered to go down to the tavern and get him home if possible. During the time they were away the guns were cleaned and loaded, the plan of defence determined on. Axes were brought in from the wood pile, forks from the barn, and stable all the wood that could be conveniently stored away in the house, a supply of water from the well. The women were instructed in loading the guns, and how they were to use an axe in certain cases if the Indians got into the house or succeeded in setting fire to it.

Ludwig Wideman

After these preliminary plans were decided on the conversation naturally drifted away to the anticipated battle. Who of the parties they knew that had gone down to join Mackenzie's army would run away, and who would stand and be shot. Philip spoke up and said, "I know one man that won't run away. If Mackenzie and all his men run away, he will stand, that man is Lude Wideman. I know the kind of man he is."

When the boys returned with young Phil they had a very tragic story to tell. While they were at the tavern Thomas Maclean of the sixth of Whitchurch drove up to the barroom door in a light wagon and called to parties to come out and see the corpse of his dear Brother-in-law. Lying on the bottom of the wagon a coarse[318] sheet over him a bullet hole[319] in his forehead the size of a quarter dollar was all that was [105] mortal of Ludwick Wideman. This report caused great sorrow in the company. They seemed to feel as if irreparable calamity had befallen the neighborhood.

Ludwick Wideman had been one of the early York pioneers. A man of more than ordinary ability, kind and generous, at all times ready to assist the needy in the many difficulties incidental to new settlers. He was the owner of at least three hundred acres of excellent land. In 1837 he was in comparison to the general settler a wealthy man. He was Captain Wideman in the York militia and through the wars of 1812–13. To those who

---

317. Paul Shell (Schell; 1805–1890) married Catherine Gower on September 11, 1832. They had three children, Joshua, Nicholas and Israel.

318. AB "course."

319. AB "wholly."

sympathized with the reform party or rather the party opposed to Government by [F]amily Compact, for they ignored the name of rebels, he was lamented as a martyr. He had sacrificed his life to obtain that which every true lover of his country hold[s] dear, government by impartial justice. What was really denied by the Family Compact and the indifference of the Colonial office. To those who had no sympathy with the reform party he was lamented for his temerity in taking up arms and leading men to fight against a government that had at least been paternal to him.

Mohawk Valley Stories

The death of Captain Wideman changed the train of thought in the company to days of long ago. Philip Gower when quite a young man came to Upper Canada from the banks of the [S]usquehanna [R]iver near Wyoming the scene of the horrible massacre perpetuated by the Mohawks[320] and Oneidas,[321] as depicted by the poet Campbell in his beautiful tale of Gertrude of Wyoming.[322] Many were still alive when Philip was a young man who were eyewitness[s]es and sufferers from that heart rending scene of atrocities by the [S]ix [N]ation Indians.[323] It was of little consequence to the Iroquois[324] whether a family was on the side of King George Washington so long as they **[105]** got the bounty for the scalp.[325] The ruthless hand of time does much to qualify and almost obliterate animosities. But it lives long in the hearts of those whose ancestors, even to future generations, were scalped, murdered and their homes despoiled. Was it any wonder that the sons and daughters, grandsons and granddaughters of those who had been victims of those hell hounds of cruelty to be anything but hostile in heart to the Government whose decree was more in accordance with Medieval times than the closing of the eighte[e]nth century.

---

320. AB "Mohahawks."

321. AB "Oneydas" here and elsewhere.

322. See Back Stories in this chapter.

323. It is at least as likely that these "atrocities" were committed by the Loyalist militia under Colonel John Butler. And the Patriot retaliation was even more hideous (see Back Stories in this chapter).

324. AB "Iroquious."

325. This is said more from prejudice than any evidence, the prejudice here probably reflecting what Uncle Alex heard from Philip Gower. And it should be remembered that both sides in the Revolutionary War put a bounty on scalps.

Back Stories of Chapter Twelve

Ludwig/Ludwick Wideman (1781–1837): Martyr to the Cause of Canadian Liberty

Ludwig's grandfather, Jacob Henry Wideman (1720–97), presumably from what would become Germany, settled in Pennsylvania in 1737. His son Philip (1749–1833) moved north to establish a farm in Markham Township in 1805, the year of the death of his wife Anna Sara (1759–1805). Some of Philip's children came with him including Ludwig. Ludwig's first wife Christiana (1791–1813) died at 22. His second wife, Elizabeth Macklem (1797–1852), like Ludwig, was born in Pennsylvania. They had six children, the last of whom, John, died in infancy.

Ludwig quickly established himself as a successful farmer, and when the War of 1812 began, he enlisted. In the apt words of Newmarket historian Robert Carter:

> Ludwick Wideman had proven his patriotism on the battlefield during the War of 1812, where he served two years as a sergeant and then ensign in Peter Robinson's Rifle Company ... a unit of the 1st York Militia raised by the eldest of Newmarket's Robinson brothers and it took part in many key battles of the war including Detroit, Queenston Heights, York and Fort Michilimakinac.

Later during the war, Wideman served under various militia captains as an acting-lieutenant. On June 12, 1818 he was promoted from ensign to lieutenant and then served in the militia until the late 1820s (Carter 2014: 44).

After the war, he came to be supportive of reformist issues, not a surprise as he wasn't English, nor did he belong to the powerful Anglican Church. Still, his radicalism did not emerge until the election of 1836. In the words of John Charles Dent (1841–1888), an English-born early Canadian journalist and historian who had interviewed Ludwig's son Philip, we can see why:

> During that election he rode to Newmarket to exercise his franchise, but as he was known to be a Reformer the strongest attempts were made to prevent him from voting. Notwithstanding the he was known to have resided on his farm for more than thirty years, and he had spent two years fighting for his country at the time of her utmost need, a demand was made that he should take the oath of allegiance. He felt all the just indignation which such treatment might be expect to arouse, and from that time forward was prepared to adopt any and every means to destroy the domina-

tion of the Compact which had the Lieutenant-Governor under its thumb. This it was which goaded him into rebellion. His memory is tenderly cherished by his descendants, who regard him as a martyr to the cause of Canadian liberty (Dent 1885: 137).

At age 56, he died of a bullet through the forehead in the skirmish at Montgomery's Tavern on December 7, 1837, and his brother-in-law drove him home in the back of a wagon to be buried near his home, in what is now the Dickson's Hill cemetery near the northern end of Markham Township.

Gertrude of Wyoming: A Pennsylvania Tale

Gertrude of Wyoming: A Pennsylvania Tale was written by Scottish poet Thomas Campbell (1777–1844), and published in 1809. It is typical of what we might call the overblown tragic romantic poetry that was popular in its day. It contains 92 nine-line stanzas. It is very difficult for this 21st century reader of poetry to get any sense from or appreciate it at any level. I have read it several times and I am still confused by the storyline. It contains many inaccuracies, including references to crocodiles and condors, and blaming "the Monster Brandt" (Mohawk leader Joseph Brant) who was not involved with the battle. This aside, it had a profound effect at the time, even being involved with the naming of the state of Wyoming.

Use of the Term Massacre: The Battle of Wyoming, the Battle of Cherry Valley and the Sullivan-Clinton Expedition

The Battle of Wyoming, Pennsylvania took place on July 3, 1788. The Loyalist militia (led by Colonel John Butler) and Seneca forces numbered around 1,000 fighters, each contributing around 500 members. They significantly outnumbered the Continental Patriot forces, and won easily. Butler claimed that many Patriot scalps were collected. I suspect that probably as many were taken by the Loyalists as by the Seneca. The battle is often termed a "massacre," which typically happens when Aboriginal forces win and settlers or soldiers are killed. It is a one-sided term.

The term "massacre" is also used to refer to the battle that took place in the village of Cherry Valley, New York on November 11, 1778. It was built around a fort. The American Continental or Patriot forces numbered 250 men but their effectiveness in defence was limited in that they were billeted in the community and did not stay in the fort, which had no barracks. To make matters worse, when soldier made it to the fort, there were no good locations from which to fire. Walter Butler, son of John Butler, brought with him 300 Rangers, the Seneca added about 400 more. Joseph Brant (this time present in the battle) brought with him about 60 more Mohawk warriors, but his loyalties were severely divided in this battle. He had friends in Cherry Valley, and acted to lessen the brutal treatment of prisoners by the others, although outnumbered, to small effect. Some 130 dead were scattered throughout the burned remains of the village. The fort remained standing with soldiers inside. For an account of the battle, see Berleth 2010: 266–273 (but remember the evidence and language used reflects one side's view).

The term "massacre" wasn't used when Patriot troops under Major General John Sullivan and Brigadier James Clinton pursued a brutal raid of retaliation in the summer of 1789. Around 40 Haudenosaunee (Six Nations Iroquois) communities were destroyed, many people (men, women and children) were killed, their stocks of corn destroyed and their fields burned. It is difficult to determine how many died of starvation or freezing over the next year, as many fled what had been their homeland for hundreds of years. I am sure that the number would have easily exceeded the casualties of both the Battle of Wyoming and the Battle of Cherry Valley put together. This is a massacre too.

Chapter Thirteen[326]
The Indian Raid and the Story of the Schells (Shells) in the Mohawk Valley

The people of the Mohawk Valley had their tales of rapine and murder even more horrible if possible than the Wyoming slaughter, in the fertile Valley of the Mohawk when the country around Utica was almost a primeval forest in Revolutionary times. A family by the name of Shell (of whom Paul already mentioned was a descendent) had settled and were busy clearing their farm as fast as time and strength would permit. They had built a good substantial log house but in the meantime [which] was covered with bark, until circumstances enabled them to get it shingled. Those who have observed the growth of young sprouts around the roots of stumps like a small copse the following year after clears, especially basswood, can to some extent realize the extreme precaution that had to be exercised by settlers in isolated districts for self preservation against the subtle[327] schemes of the Indian. The Indians would collect a number of branches with leaves so like those around stumps, and, crawling among the stumps holding before them this improvised deception, would get within gun shot where the family were working in their clearing, and yelling their demonic war [w]hoop rush upon their unsuspecting victims, scalp and murder them before they could reach the shelter of their house. Occasionally it [**107**] was the house that was attacked when the man and his wife and under branches of the family were out in the clearing at work, when the younger children would be scalped or stolen away.[328] Experience had taught these settlers that before commencing their labour to take their guns with them, and beat around the stumps and edge [of] the woods along the clearing in case the Indians were skulking around. It must be remembered that the Revolutionary [W]ar lasted from 1775 to 1781.

But as is often the case with the most astute strategists precaution for once was neglected by the Shells, and the consequences were an experience endured by them never to be forgotten. The father, mother and eldest son Ben (a lad of fourteen or sixteen years) neglected the customary supervision, had not heard of Indians being on the war path for some months. On a beautiful June morning [they] went out to hoe their corn. They had scarcely commenced their work when a band of Indians burst upon them with fiendish yell. They ran towards their house, impelled to speed by the

---

326. This is chapter 11 in the original manuscript.

327. AB "subtile."

328. See Back Stories in this chapter. The scalping and killing of children was greatly exaggerated. Captured settler children were usually adopted and raised by the people.

fact that their younger children were around the house and clearing, than by the bullets that whistled around them as they ran zigzag to spoil the aim of the Indians. As they neared the house the father picked up a child in each hand. Ben another cheering on the mother in the race with all the comforting words the exigency of the case inspired them. Close by the home, a little girl two or three years old was playing almost under a large kettle set on edge. The man could not stoop to pick her up, but trailed his foot over the kettle completely covering the child. This little girl [was] almost miraculously saved, for she did not cry, and the Indians suspected nothing under the kettle. She was in 1837 an old lady, mother of a large family living with her son David March not over a mile from our house. I have seen her often. To my recollection she was a medium sized lady, **[108]** fair and pleasant to look upon. Think she could only converse in her native Dutch,[329] but would welcome you with a pleasant smile and <u>So be gaites</u>.

Well they got into their house and barricaded the door, and windows as secure as possible. Two boys were missing Mark and Fred.[330] They were taken by the Oneidas who were more merciful [than] the renegade white men (called <u>tories</u> by the continentals) who would have blown the lads' brains out had not a powerful Oneida dashed aside the gun and with uplifted tomahawk would have given these malefactors a quick passport to eternity, but his hand was staid by the other Indians. This fine specimen of his tribe protected and befriended the boys, often when tired carried them on his back a piece on the way until safely delivered to the British arm. Then taken to Quebec where they were kept in a kind of Orphanage. They got some education, learned trades but never saw their parents again. However, after many years they were united to their kinsfolk in Markham. In 1837 Mark owned an excellent farm in Markham and occasionally wrought at his trade, a tailor. He was a man of good mental ability and for his opportunities very intelligent. He had been very observant of all he saw and heard during the journey from the Mohawk Valley to Quebec, and then to Markham. In 1840 he was well stricken in years. I have conversed with him when a boy on his experience with the red men. He once rode in our wagon with Jamie and me from Toronto to Reid's Corners.[331] We were good listeners, he was a good and willing talker so the enjoyment was mutual. He did not seem to entertain great animosity towards the Indians. He said the Oneidas were very kind to them, given the best of food they had, and, as a great part of the journey was through a trackless forest, they were often weary and fell behind, but it did not seem an extra burden to the Oneidas to throw them on their backs and march on in Indian file one behind the other. To the renegade white men that generally accompanied the Indians

329. That is, she spoke in German.
330. I think his name was Henry.
331. Later known as Victoria Square.

he poured out the [109] vials of his wrath in vocables perhaps pertinent to occasion but certainly rather pungent. He knew all about Grenville[']s Stamp Act,[332] three pence per pound on tea and said it was the most puerile legislation outside of an Absolute Government.

But to return to the subject of defence in case the Indians did come, several new stratagems were proposed but the conversation would revert to anecdotes on the sufferings of their people during the revolutionary war. The Shells, after getting into their house and fortifying it as well as circumstances would permit. It was do or die in the attempt to save themselves and children. They were six miles from a blockhouse where they could expect any relief. They had to economize [on] ammunition, food and water as they might be besieged several days, only shooting through the cracks between the logs of their house when sure of their mark. Often they thought the Indians had retired but when they ventured out to obtain water their apparent withdrawal was only a feint to attack them without danger to themselves. After a prolonged waiting and thinking they certainly had retired for good Mrs Shell stood up on some improvised platform to a higher and wider crack to recon[no]itre when a bullet passed through her hair grazing the top of her head. For three days and night this family defended themselves. They were faint for lack of food, water and sleep. Their[333] only chance for life was to prevent the Indians from getting near enough to set fire to the roof of their house now being as dry as tinder. This had been attempt[ed] several times and failed. It must be borne in mind that the early settlers in the American Colonies previous to and during revolutionary times were expert marksmen with the long smooth bore rifle, which assisted the Colonists very much in the revolutionary battles. The Kentucky men were cunning hunters, and brave soldiers and dead shots with their long rifle. Fortunately for the Shells they had two rifles [110] of the old Colonial regime. A young man's first investment was a rifle. In the old Colonial times when the early colonists had to defend themselves against Indians and wild beasts, to be a good marksman was a necessary adjunct in the qualification of a settler. Young Ben was a crack marksman, so was his father and they knew the cunning traits of the red men, and the cowardly nature of the white men that accompanied them. They would not risk their life if they could avoid it but they were the first to plunder. Whenever an Indian ventured from behind a tree or stump it was immediate exit to the happy hunting ground[334] beyond the setting sun. [B]efore they could make

---

332. See Back Stories in this chapter.

333. AB "There chances of life."

334. The expression "happy hunting ground" was not part of the culture of the Aboriginal nations in Upper Canada. It is more associated with Plains people, particularly the Oglala Sioux, and was popularized in the Western frontier literature of the late 19th and early 20th century. This is probably where Uncle Alex learned the phrase.

a rush towards the house the other rifle was reloaded. The mother kept one rifle always ready. Finding that help was coming from the block house the Indians became exasperated, having[335] failed so many times and [having] lost a number of braves, made a furious onset and succeeded in throwing fire brands on the roof of their house. At this unfortunate crisis all hope seemed vain, when woman's wit proved more effective than the unening [?] rifle. A hive of bees was sheltered at one end of the house. Mrs Shell thrust a stick through a crack and upset the hive. As a matter of course the bees attacked[336] the Indians, who fled pell mell to the forest and [at] this juncture help arrived from the block house and the Shells were saved, but the two little boys were gone.

Many tales of deeds too fiendish and horrible for imagination to conceive were indulged in during the evening. The Butler Rangers were denounced as being more fiendish in their modes of torture than the Indians. To stab a bayonet in the body of a little child, hold it above their heads and enjoy the child writing in agony, called it kicking the frog. Sticking splints into the breasts of women and setting fire to them. Tomahawking babies in the cradle. Nor was scalping and murder all the heart-rendering atrocities of white men. Even by Indians [111] such cruelties are[337] hard to conceive under any condition. But to be winked at by British Statesmen seems to be a tale only conceivable in the wars of Atil[l]a. It was told of a family who had retired a short distance from their house to perform some necessary work leaving their baby asleep in the cradle. Indians had been lurking around on the watch, seized the opportunity and rushed upon the house. A squaw drew her tomahawk to sink it in the baby's head, the baby smiled and reached up its hands to be lifted out of the cradle. Mother nature overcame the savage, she carried the child away to her forest home and adopted her as a daughter Indian fashion, but she really was a slave.[338] This baby a young woman when she escaped from her Indian mother, her parents were dead. Ravishing young girls was by no means uncommon. How many parents and innocent children were thus sacrificed to the almost idiotic policy of King George and his Cabinet to the American Colonists.

The above is a specimen of the stories told at Philip's kitchen fire during the evening of the Casus belli.[339] About midnight I was put to bed with my sister in a large wide bed, closely curtained, in a corner of the store room. The girl was soon in the land of Nod,[340] but I had heard too much about

---

335. AB "have."

336. AB "attackted" here and elsewhere.

337. AB "is."

338. The literature on captured and adopted children suggests otherwise. See Back Stories in this chapter.

339. AB "Casesus." The Latin term as spelled in the text above means "case for war."

340. An imaginary land of sleep.

scalping and murder to sleep, and was by no means reconciled that our lives were out of danger. Although no fugitives from the attacked houses had come our way.

The Dutch people at this time slept with a feather bed above as well as below. I did not like it. I felt very uncomfortable. I rose dressed as best I could and found my way back to the kitchen. My father ordered me back to the bed again, [telling me] that I would be in the way if anything happened, but the old lady of the house interposed. She said I might be useful. She produced a large knife half way between a butcher knife and a carving knife, gave it to me and in her best nasal [112] twang said, "If the Ingins come and you see my old man or your daddie fittin an Ingin you get behind the Ingin, and shove the knife in here." Pointing to her left side under her heart, "Send it right up." I took the knife with the intention of following her instruction if need be. I have no thought that this unsophisticated old lady knew anything of the science of anatomy although she practised as a Midwife for many miles around but she knew where the fifth was, just as well as Joab[341] did, King David's celebrated general, and he was no novice at the business.

I was placed to watch a window looking west on the Townline. I was told if I saw anything even a shadow on the road I was to call "I see something." Philip gave orders that no one was to shout or go outside until he gave orders. About two o'clock I observed something like men move in the distance. I gave the alarm. All came and looked at the moving figures eagerly, now quite visible. It was now quite evident a crisis was at hand. Each one grasped his or her weapon. It was a fight for dear life. After scrutinizing the men a few minutes for they were now distinct in the starlight. Philip said "them ain't Ingins, them are white men. I know an Ingin as far as I can see him." But other[s] in the company were not so sanguine of their being white men. When in full view it was observed they carried guns. Men at this time if they did wear and overcoat it was made[e] of home manufactured cloth, dyed[342] with butternut bark. Those coats had a number of tippets on the shoulders diminishing in size up to the neck. They were long down to the ankles[343], and in the dim light had the appearance of the blanket coat of an Indian. Hence the suspicion[344] of they're[345] not being white men after all. The subtle devices of the red men had often caused much tribulation on the banks of the Mohawk and Susquehanna, and extreme [113] caution

---

341. Joab was a nephew of King David and for a while the commander of his army. In the King James Version of the Bible (2 Samuel 20:10) he stabs Amasa, his cousin, with a knife in his fifth rib. More recent versions of the Bible just refer to him stabbing him in the stomach.

342. AB "died."

343. AB "ancles."

344. AB "supicion."

345. AB "there."

was observed to the last. The men came around the house to the kitchen door. As they came the guns were pointed toward the door. It was evident now they were white men as they knew the way and came suspecting no danger. Still fear was not allayed. The acme of our peril would be decided in an instant either in tragedy[346] or comedy. The men knocked at the door. Philip opened it and the men walked in. They laughed at the preparations to meet them and the Indians, but immediately became quite serious, and said "This will never do." The men were well known. James Lloyd and Reuben Mills, they had come nearly four miles to warn us and others in the neighborhood to meet at a certain place tomorrow, or as soon as possible and build a blockhouse and get the women and children into it. After much controversy for and against building the block house it was final[l]y agreed that if tomorrow's information was a confirmation that Indians had been, or were now on the war path then certainly build the blockhouse, if not every man stay at home and mind his own business.

How this false alarm originated and got abroad was never really known. Some alleged it started from a band of Indians marching down Yonge Street from Snake Island in feathers and war paint to help the Government. Others say it [was] started by people along Yonge St. who had relatives with Mackenzie and raised this hue and cry to give pretext they were out armed for protection against the Indians for fear of being arrested. In our neighborhood the report came almost five o'clock. How far it travelled eastward we never heard but we learned in a few days that as it travelled to the east it became more frightful. Families who had retired for the night got up and ran, they knew not whither, half clad in an intensely [114] cold night, or early morning. Bright star light. The trees in the woods snapping like rifle shots.

The great majority who participated in this Scare have gone beyond the veil[347] that separates[348] time from eternity. Those that are alive and can remember it are old men and old women, who can look back on nearly seventy years ago and wonder at the change as a dream or hallucination instead of a stern reality.

Back Stories of Chapter Thirteen

The Indian Raid

Chief William Yellowhead or Musquakie of the Anishinaabe or Ojibwa in response to a request/order from Governor Francis Bond Head led a group of Anishinaabe warriors down Yonge Street to Toronto. At the time three Anishinaabe bands were living together in an area known as The Nar-

346. AB "tradegy."

347. AB "vail."

348. AB "seperates," here and elsewhere.

rows in and around present day Orillia. Government pressure had brought them there to learn farming in 1830. By the end of the decade white settler pressure for their land would drive them off into three separate communities: Rama, Snake Island and Christian Island. Yellowhead was recognized as a leader by Bond Head as he and his father were well-known veterans of the War of 1812. He was the chief of the Rama band. Chief Joseph Snake was the leader of the Snake Island band (who would later move to nearby Georgina Island in southern Lake Simcoe), and Chief John Assance led the people who went to Beausoleil Island, later to nearby Christian Island, near the south shore of Georgian Bay.

Yellowhead and his warriors, whose exact numbers and band contribution do not seem to be known, arrived at the scene of the showdown on Yonge Street by the Montgomery Inn, but the battle was over. Their presence there would have been an effective deterrent to further rebel action.

As Bond Head was concerned about the rebels who lived in the Holland Landing area (including Bradford and Sharon), what is today a short drive north of Toronto, he asked Yellowhead and his men to winter there. In da Silva and Hind's excellent chapter "Chief Yellowhead and Natives," in *Rebels against Tories in Upper Canada 1837,* the hard circumstances faced by those people who would then and years later learn to distrust the name of Bond Head are well described:

> They were unable to do their winter hunting, so were reliant upon the government to tend to their needs. However, pay and provisions suddenly stopped arriving after only a few weeks, leaving the Indians in dire straits as food ran desperately short. Though a proud man, Yellowhead was forced to petition the government for supplies, claiming that his people were at risk of starvation unless they got immediate relief. Finally, food began to arrive and the immediate danger passed, but the combination of biting cold and utter boredom made for a dreadful existence (Da Silva and Hind 2010: 68).

So the causes of the belief in "the Indian Raid," as I am calling it, were threefold. There was a heightened anxiety brought on by the Rebellion. A kind of civil war brings about a lack of trust in the way things appear, and in the nature of the people around you. Second, there were armed Aboriginal people walking down Yonge Street in settler country north of Toronto. And finally, there were a good number of settlers who had directly experienced or heard from their parents of real danger with Aboriginal people (not Anishinaabe) and Butler's Rangers, an often brutal Loyalist militia, in Pennsylvania and New York during the American Revolution. Their stories inflamed the sparks of apprehension into a raging fire of false fears.

The Treatment of White Prisoners

The stories of the torture and scalping of women and children are exaggerated in stories of settler battles in which Aboriginal people were involved, while adoption has long been downplayed or ignored. In my own work researching and writing *The Eighteenth Century Wyandot: A Clan Based Study* (Steckley 2014), I found that children and women captured from the Fox people whom the Wyandot were fighting were adopted into the society. There was a flurry of baptisms (with Wyandot godparents) of both groups. And one Fox woman became a respected Wyandot elder.

The Stamp Act

The Stamp Act of 1765 was enacted by British Prime Minister George Grenville. It required documents (and even playing cards) to be issued on paper manufactured and stamped (as proof of origin) in Britain, and paid for with British money, not the money of the colonies. One of its main functions was to pay for the continued presence of British soldiers on American soil after the war known variously as the Seven Years War (1756–63), the French and Indian War (in the U.S.), and the War of the Conquest (in Canada). It was repealed the next year but set a precedent of unreasonable taxes and colonial resistance.

Chapter Fourteen
Mackenzie's Men

When daylight came each one resumed his bundle and we trudged away back through the snow and stumps to our old house again. As we drew near, perhaps a hundred yards from it three man were approaching from the west, guns on their shoulders. It was a matter of doubt who would reach the house first. The men increased their speed and reached the door as soon as we did. I have no recollection that they said one word to my father, or that he spoke to them, but as soon as the door was opened they rushed in set their guns down but[t]s on the floor and whispered to each other. Then the eldest man said:

"We are three of Mackenzie's men; we've been at the battle; we ran away up the west side of Yonge Street. We crossed it in the night. We have come through woods, swamps, and fields; houses are abandoned and locked against us. We are terrible hungry. We must have something to eat."

My mother answered, "If you sit down peace[a]bly until we get the fire going and I get some food cooked you shall have it." The oldest man said "Our lives are in your hands, but we trust in your generosity. Are you a Mackenzie man?"

My father answered him emphatically:

"No. Mackenzie and his party have been spearing at a windmill. Notwithstanding that Mackenzie has been much abused by the family compact, and the great need of reform in the [115] Executive of the country. The country in the meantime is governed by a petty Oligarchy there is little doubt and a new order of management of affairs must come in the near future, but not rebellion at the present by Mr. Mackenzie. Mackenzie and his party imported aid from the neighboring Republic, but the American Government know better than risk a war with Britain on such trivial and indefinite conditions as Mackenzie and Papineau could offer. The insurgent party have no means to carry on war. They have no credit. Evidently the majority of the people are not in favour of taking arms to break the power of the family compact. With few exceptions the population of Upper Canada are eager for reform in the Governmental affairs of the country, but the events of yesterday proved they hesitated before engaging in rebellion. Mr Mackenzie is honest in his convictions but has made an egregious mistake. He will have brought trouble and death to many families by causing rebellion. He has aroused the feelings of a certain class of people by his inflame[m]atory harangues against the powers that be. True no doubt to a large extent but his remedy has been Utopian. He is no George Washington. Moreover what would undi[s]ciplined men like you do to repel even a few regular troops? Yo[u] have neither weapons nor the means of procuring them. You have nothing worthy of the name of munitions of war.

Lifting one of their guns he said:

"Where is your bayonet? This thing is a mere toy simply a boy's fowling piece, would scarcely wound a man at fifty yards. A company of regulars would put a thousand of you Hors de combat in a few minutes. You many have Spartan courage but you lack almost everything else. Perhaps you thought to get rich much faster by serving Mars[349] than being the rural husbandman. You would better go to your farms and resume the axe and han[d]spike."

The men stood open [116] mouthed during this rather discouraging view of the Mackenzie party. The spokesman of the two said, "I guess you're[350] about right Mister."

They told how they had been duped, coaxed away to a meeting, were not allowed to go home again, some one was sent back for their guns. They were much afraid of being taken prisoners, they knew the penalty for high treason was death.

These men belonged to the township of Brock at least fifty miles from our place and seventy five from Toronto. They had walked all this distance, sure of taking the then Capital of Upper Canada, get much spoil and on their way back, select the best farms of those who were not Mackenzie men and appropriate them to themselves.

Doubtless there were[351] men of good mental ability engaged in the rebellion of 1837, but none turned up to indicate a leader or military genius. The same class of men did not live in Canada, at least in Upper Canada as the American Colonists in the time of the revolution, at least not many of them. They had defended themselves for many years against the attacks of hostile Indians. They had a large experience in warfare. The Colonial Militia had fought the veterans of France. The New England States were peopled by a stock of rare fighting qualities descendents of the men or class of men that composed Cromwell's Ironsides.[352] During the Commonwealth the English army and navy were almost invincible. The men of the Southern States were descendents[353] of the loyal Cavaliers[354] who were men of war by profession, proud of their patrician decent and nobility. In 1835 and 1837 the great majority of the people in Upper Canada were American settlers and descendents who had emigrated from the new Republic. And an industrious class of farmers and farm laborers, also mechanics from the

---

349. The Roman god of war.

350. AB "your."

351. AB "was."

352. See Back Stories in this chapter.

353. AB "descendants."

354. See Back Stories in this chapter.

British Islands whose object was to better their circumstances in life, than engage in [117] rebellion. If the Canadian Patriots expected or trusted to a repetition of the same conditions of men and other resources in 1837 as the Americans had[355] in 1773 it was a great miscalculation.

The rabble that gathered at Mon[t]gomery's Tavern to take Toronto were not by any means the representative class of the population. The majority were weak in understanding easily duped by fair promises. Perhaps in the annals of war no greater exhibition of poltroonery is known than the flight of Mackenzie and his army from Gallows Hill. The only man we ever heard of that stood when his comrad[e]s fled was Ludwick Wideman. Now when nearly seventy years have come and gone, one cannot look back on this much to be lamented deformity of wresting the Canadas from the British Crown but feel a pang of sorrow for such men as Wideman, Lount and Matthews. Especially when we know the fact, that in a few years amnesty was granted to every one engaged in that unmitigated blunder. It must have been aggravating to the relations and friends of those who were killed or taken prisoners and hanged to know that the leaders returned again, were elected and sat in the parliament of Canada.

The Rebellion Losses Bill

All through the winter of 1838 there was ill feeling and recrimination among the people. Every day or two we heard of a warrant being out for this one, or the next one. My father and mother often felt uneasy as they fed and harboured rebels.[356] Men claiming to have commission from government tramped the County, taking people's guns, seizing horses under the plea of having authority to do so. These men may likely have been loyal insofar as taking farmers' teams and sleighs or saddles, to drive a ten or twelve miles when the government interest might be one, and their <u>own nine</u>. At all events few of these men possessed the essentials of what is considered good citizenship in 1906. In some cases and [118] in some parts of the country there were[357] actual cases of government authority for the seizure of hidden armour[358] if found in the possession of suspected parties, also to take a team if required, but in our neighbourhood the authority was used more as a matter of spite than government requirement. It was simply marauding.

The above mentioned abuses and others of a like nature were[359] the cause of the beginning of the Rebellion Losses Bill being brought before

---

355. AB "did."
356. AB "rebells."
357. AB "was."
358. It is likely that he meant "armoury" here, a stash of weapons and ammunition.
359. AB "was."

parliament during Lord Cathcart's administration.[360] I think in 1845 a commission was appointed to make inquiry as to the losses sustained by individuals of such kind as I have mentioned above. The commission found that a great number of individuals who had no part nor lot in the rebellion whatever, had received serious losses and were determined to push their claims. The report of the commissioners was only partially acted upon in 1845. But in 1849 the case came before the Governor in Council, and subsequently before parliament to be final[l]y disposed of. The bill passed both houses and was assented to in the Queen's name by Lord Elgin.[361] The then Opposition (tories) rotten egged the Governor in the streets of Montreal, the government being in that city since 1844. They set fire to the houses of parliament and with the library and public records were almost totally destroyed.[362] In consequence of this extreme ebullition[363] of party feeling the seat of government was immediately removed to Toronto, and Lord Elgin tendered his resignation. The Queen however would not receive it but raised him to the Peerage.

To the young Canadians of today and for generations yet unborn this treasonable outrage may be difficult to reconcile with the vaunted loyalty evinced by the same party heretofore in Canadian history. Loyalty in power and loyalty in opposition in this case however were not in [**119**] juxtaposition. The rotten egging of the Queen's Representative was an act of extreme violence, but dishonoring of the Queen by demolishing her portrait was certainly an act that would have cost the people their heads less than two hundred years ago in British history. The fact is this uncalled for effervescence of spite, on the part of the tory party, is wholly unreconcilable with their professed principles. I have no distinct remembrance of the reasons urged by the Opposition against the bill during the debate, but the fact that the bill was passed by a reform government was an acknowledgement by the electorate[364] of the country that malevolence and gross recklessness by the government officials previous to and during the rebellion campaign

---

360. Charles Murray Cathcart (1783–1859) was Governor of the united provinces of Upper and Lower Canada from April 1846 to January 1847.

361. James Bruce (1811–63), the eighth Earl of Elgin, was appointed Governor in 1847 and held the position until 1854. He became a target of conflict in 1849 with his giving royal assent to the Rebellion Losses Bill. This led him to distancing his position from that of the legislature.

362. For a discussion of this series of actions see John Turing (2016), "Conservatives and conditional loyalty: The Rebellion Losses crisis of 1849 in Montreal," *British Journal of Canadian Studies* 29(1): 83–103.

363. AB "ebullution." While this word literally refers to boiling and bubbling, it can refer, in cases such as this, to a sudden outburst of emotion or violence.

364. AB "electoral."

had been wholly unworthy and in many cases unnecessarily[365] severe. It seemed to be taken for granted by the tory party, or I might say more properly the Orange[366] party in the county, that if a man did not pose in some way to manifest his loyalty as a very obsequious loyalist, as a sergeant, a Captain, a Colonel, or make some great demonstration of his love to the family compact party he was a rebel sympathizer and that was enough to evoke the spleen of the men who stayed[367] at home and paid strict attention to their own business.

In the spring of 1838 one day a young man rode up to our house and inquired for my father, he was away at some distance from the house. My mother asked him if he particularly washed to see him. He handed her a paper. She read the preamble and said, "Yes, I am sure he would sign it, if he were here. I will sign it for him if you have no objections." He thanked her. This was a son of Samuel Lount's getting petitions for his father's life. But although signed by nearly everyone in North York, it evoked no compassion [120] in the heart of Sir George Arthur.[368] The late judge Lount was a grandson of the unfortunate Samuel.[369]

My narrative has grown much longer than I intended when I began. It might be extended still further, as my memory recalls many incidents in connection with the rebellion, and its antecedents, for it was not a crisis of phenomenal growth, but it is perhaps too long already and not very interesting to young people, perhaps only to those who can remember events as they passed along.

A Trip to Toronto in 1839

In the month of May 1839, I accompanied my father and mother to Toronto, with a load of various farm produce to sell.[370] The rebellion agitation was not all subsided, there was a vast [amount] to sold[i]er[r]ing going on in the city. There appeared to be as many men in various uniforms moving around in the market as there were in civilians'. Can remember quite well the appearance of the scene of the battle field, if it was worthy of the name as it appeared then. It was said everything was just about the same as when the contending parties left. The ruins of Mon[t]gomery's Tavern, Dr.

---

365. AB "unnecessary."

366. See Back Stories in this chapter (The Orange Party).

367. AB "staid."

368. See Back Stories in this chapter (Sir George Arthur).

369. Judge William Lount (1840–1903) was the son of Samuel's brother George, and thus a nephew, not his grandson. He was born in Holland Landing. He became a lawyer, represented Simcoe North in the first provincial parliament of Ontario, and Toronto Centre as a Liberal in the federal Parliament. He was appointed a judge in 1901.

370. AB "sale."

Horn's house,[371] Gibson's house,[372] the clump of pines, southwest of the tavern ruins, the wagon makers' shop a cannon ball went through, bullet holes through windows, along the street towards Yorkville. Almost opposite the tavern ruins, and near the middle of the street was pointed out the spot where Colonel Moodie fell. This officer was retired on half pay.[373] The Colonel and Captain Stewart[374] were riding to town to assist the Government. The rebels or at least a party of them, formed in the street ostensibly to take them prisoners. Captain Stewart called the Colonel's attention to the movement, but the Colonel despised them as unworthy of parley, and said "We'll rid[e] through them." Spurring their horses to a gallop, they dashed on the group of men on the street. It was alleged by some of the parties on the street that the Colonel fired a [121] pistol. At that juncture the sharp crack of a rifle rang from the barroom door, and Colonel Moodie fell from his horse dead. This small and insignificant foe proved fatal to the hero of many battles. It was said the Colonel acted rashly, no doubt he did. I never heard that the parties who attempted to take them prisoners had orders from whoever was their officer in command at the tavern. Neither did I ever hear if they knew who the Colonel and Captain Stewart were.

The readers of Canadian history will doubtless be impressed that Colonel Moodie died an ignoble death. He fought as a young officer with Sir Ralph Abercrom[b]ie at the landing in Egypt below Alexandria on the banks of the Nile, just one hundred and five years ago 21st of last March. When the British army first measured themselves with the veterans of Republican France, and proved they were perfectly able to cope with the troops that had made all Europe to resound. General Menou and his [In]vincibles were routed with great slaughter, and brave old General Abercrom[b]ie in his eightieth year was killed.[375] It may be irregular to mention here but I cannot refrain from quoting a few lines of a song of this battle sung by my father. Never saw it in print.[376] Never heard it sung by anyone but himself. What I remember of it is as follows:

Many a brave General Britannia can boast.
And many to it too true, by their lives are lost,
Among them Abercrom[b]ie, who may be ranked now.
Who lost his life in Egypt, fighting with Menou

371. See Back Stories in this chapter (Dr. Robert Horne).

372. See Back Stories in this chapter (David Gibson).

373. See Back Stories in this chapter (Colonel Moodie).

374. This was Captain Hugh Stewart, once of the Royal Navy (Berchem 1996: 141).

375. Ralph Abercrombie (1734–1801) died as the result of the Battle of Alexandria in his 67th year.

376. I have been unable to find this song in print either. Perhaps Uncle Alex's father was trying his hand at poetry, and this piece was never published.

Tis of this bloody battle these[377] few lines I have wrote
To tell you how this morning he got his fatal stroke,
Twas on[378] the twenty first of March, eighteen hundred and one,
As we were standing by our arms before daylight came on,
The French came stealing on us to catch us by surprise [122]
But we gave them a volley which quickly opened their eyes,
Upon our left they did engage, a grand attack to make,
They thought if it was possible, our front lines they would break,
But our brave British heroes to fly they did disdain,
Each man in Frenchman's blood they did their bayonets stain,
But now the clouds were darkening, no slackness to be found
While many a tender mother's son lay bleeding on the ground,
But how can I make mention how does my spirits drown,
Brave General Abercrom[b]ie received a mortal wound
Two men supporting him, with the spyglass in his hand,
Midst clouds of smoke, and shell and shots, still giving the command.

I have not heard these lines sung or quoted but by myself for over sixty years. They are incomplete, and not in proper measure. There are[379] a few lines more but I cannot get them to rhyme proper. I have seen and heard an old soldier tell of this battle before we left Scotland. The two famous Highland regiments were at this battle. The old man I refer to was sergeant McGowan of the 92nd raised by the Dutches[s] of Gordon, the other the famous black watch or 42nd.

Colonel Moodie likewise served with Sir John Moore in his campaign in Spain, and the famous retreat to Corun[n]a.[380] He had faced the most famous veteran troops of modern times, and to lose his life on Yonge Street either by his own rashness, or someone acting under impulse, without order or authority was humiliating indeed. I never heard any clear and concise statement of the occurrence. He was not shot by any of the men that formed in the street apparently to take him prisoner. The fatal shot was fired from the <u>barroom</u> door. It was not war but simply murder.

Many vague reports went around the county, as to who fired the fatal shot. No one was ever mentioned by name, so far as I can remember. It was rumored [123] in 1839 that the man who shot the Colonel spent a year and a half in the woods in (the now) neighbourhood Co[l]lingwood and Owen Sound.

377. AB "this."

378. AB "one."

379. AB "is."

380. Scottish born Lieutenant General John Moore (1761–1809) fought the French in Spain, and was fatally injured at the Battle of Corunna. There was a then famous poem written about it.

The Memoirs of Alexander Brodie

BACK STORIES OF CHAPTER FOURTEEN

Cromwell's Ironsides

The twenty year period from 1640 to 1660 is known as the time of the English Civil Wars and the Commonwealth. Parliament led by Oliver Cromwell rose up against the Catholic king, Charles I, ending with the beheading of the king in 1649. The people who supported the king were called Cavaliers. There followed the ten year period of the Commonwealth, with Cromwell at the head. Ironsides was the name given to Cromwell's cavalry, after Cromwell's nickname, "Ironside." His army and a good number of his supporters were Puritans, who were guided by an extreme form of Protestantism, including a strong form of anti-Catholicism. Uncle Alex may well have romanticized them because of his own rather serious and rigid form of Presbyterianism.

Rebels
Samuel Lount

Samuel Lount (1791–1838) was one of many early settlers in Upper Canada, particularly York County, to be born in and come from Pennsylvania. Like some of them he was raised as a Quaker. He came to Whitchurch Township in 1818, eventually moving to Holland Landing in 1822. He was a social progressive, being involved in such efforts as a local farmers' co-operative, but did not become actively involved with politics until Mackenzie was forcibly expelled from the assembly. He was elected in 1834 as the representative of Simcoe County. He was not re-elected in 1836 when the election was manipulated by the Tories. He was a prominent figure in the Rebellion, second in unofficial rank to Mackenzie. Unfortunately, he and Mackenzie failed to co-ordinate their plans and forces in 1837, one major reason for their being so soundly defeated. When he was captured a popular petition (signed by 8,000 people) was circulated that asked that he be pardoned. In later years Mackenzie and the other leaders who escaped would be pardoned. But Lount was executed on April 12, 1838. His last words were: "Be of good courage, boys. I am not ashamed of anything I've done. I trust in God, and I'm going to die like a man." These words are recorded in a plaque dedicated to Lount in Holland Landing.

Peter Mathews

Peter Mathews (c. 1789–1838) was born in the Bay of Quinte area, later moving to Pickering Township where he was a farmer. He joined the militia, fighting alongside Isaac Brock as a sergeant in the War of 1812. He played an active role in the rebellion, leading 60 some men in a diversionary skirmish on the bridge that crossed the Don River. He was captured and executed along with Samuel Lount on the palisaded grounds in front of the King Street jail. As was the case with Lount, he was first buried in the Potter's Field by Yorkville (near Bloor and Yonge), later reburied in the Necropolis, in 1859, with William Lyon Mackenzie in attendance. Mackenzie would later be buried there himself.

David Gibson

David Gibson (1804–1864) was born in Scotland, and immigrated to Lower Canada in 1824. After some delay in finding work, he eventually became a deputy surveyor of roads. He established himself in a farm on Yonge Street in what is now Willowdale, in north Toronto (between Sheppard and Finch). Gibson was a moderate reformer, who was elected to the Legislative Assembly both in 1834, and in 1836 (when many reformers were voted out). Although he was relatively moderate, he joined Mackenzie at Montgomery's Tavern, where he protected the loyalist/tory prisoners and led them to safety when the tavern was attacked. Despite this move, the Lieutenant-Governor Francis Bond Head, a narrow-minded and punitive man, had Gibson's farm burned in punishment. He rose to success again, was pardoned in 1843, and the current Gibson House Museum is the house he had built in 1851,

Tories

Sir George Arthur

Sir George Arthur (1784–1854) was an officer in the British army, then a career political administrator in the British Empire who served as Lieutenant Governor of the British Honduras (now Belize), and Tasmania before being the Lieutenant Governor of Upper Canada, from March 23, 1638 to 1841. He knew little of the situation in Canada. His term in Canada was unremarkable except for his signing the execution orders of Samuel Lount and Peter Mathews. After leaving Canada, he was appointed the Governor of Bombay.

Dr. Robert Horne

The reference to "Dr. Horn's house" is to the house of Robert Charles Horne (c. 1780–1845), who had a varied career as army surgeon, printer/publisher and chief teller of the Bank of Upper Canada. He was a tory, very sympathetic to the Family Compact. It was reported that he used his position in the bank to deny financial services to William Lyon Mackenzie, and that this was the reason that Mackenzie set fire to the home on Yonge just north of Bloor (in Yorkville) on his ill-fated mission of December 7, 1837 (www.biographi.ca/en/bio/horne_robert_charles_7E.html).

Lieutenant-Colonel Robert Moodie

Lieutenant-Colonel Robert Moodie (1778–1837) was born in Scotland, and fought in several different areas in the British Army. When he fought on the British and Canadian side in the War of 1812, he began as a Major and was promoted to Lieutenant-Colonel by the time the war had ended. He was retired at half pay and went to live in Richmond Hill. He came out of retirement to be involved on the government side. He was shot to death on December 4, at the beginning of the conflicts on Yonge Street.

The Orange Party

The Loyal Orange Institution of Orange Order is a Protestant fraternal organization with a strong history of political influence in Canada, particularly Toronto. The name comes from the Protestant King William I who came from the area of Orange in the Netherlands, and whose army defeated that of the Catholic King James II in the Battle of the Boyne in 1690. The organization began in Northern Ireland, its area of greatest strength, in 1795. It was established in Upper Canada in 1830, was early involved with "Loyalist riots" and exercised significant political power there afterwards, especially in Toronto, which was nicknamed "the Belfast of Canada." Almost every mayor of that city until the early 1970s belonged to the Orange Order. Four Conservative prime ministers, beginning with John A. Macdonald and ending with John Diefenbaker, were members of the Orange Order.

Chapter Fifteen
Philip Gower

Before concluding my story I must briefly revert to my old friend Philip Gower. Unfortunately for this rare specimen of his class, he was subject to spells of dementia about every five or six years.[381] If the spell came on in the fall or beginning of winter, it passed away with warm weather and vice versa. When afflicted by this mental defect, he fancies himself a man of great ability, and wealth in the land, full of schemes for accumulating riches, fast. In his gigantic projects for becoming a Colossus in wealth and power he believed himself a kind of prototype of Cecil Rhodes.[382] Purely an imaginary Rhodes, for so far as I can remember Philip had bidden adieu to this Mundane scene before the real Rhodes was born. Nevertheless a Rhodes was in his mind's eye though still to come in the future. But unlike the Rhodes to come, his schemes never materialized. It mat[t]ered not though one scheme went agley, and a dozen failed, experience taught him nothing. No matter whether in his mental aber[r]ation or in his most lucid moments, he had an inordinate delight in setting fire to almost anything that would burn. Whether this was innate to him, I know not, but at all events he was in an ecstasy of delight when he got a whole chopping in a blaze. It might be that from his childhood, he had been so accustomed to burning, clearing land that it became a second nature to him.

Of course the getting [of] a good burn was a very important thing in clearing land, and to get a first rate burn, was of rare occurrence. Often when wind and drouth[383] were favourable and the fires blazing well either bush or log heaps, a heavy thunder shower came and drowned out the fire. It was seldom that a second burn succeeded very well. We often thought there [was] some mystic spell exorcised by Philip more than genuine skill **[124]** in getting log heaps and brush heaps to burn. It seemed only to require his presence in a chopping to have it all in a blaze.

When Philip was in his rational state of mind his statements of where he had been, what he had seen, and what he had one, were fairly reliable. But when on the ramble his stories were apt to be tinged with the marvellous, especially when he Philip became a cardinal point in the story.

The Battle of Queenston Heights

381, It could be that Philip Gower was suffering from a form of PTSD, given his intense experiences in the War of 1812.

382. Cecil Rhodes (1853–1902) was a rich colonial businessman whose company ruled what was formerly called Rhodesia (now Zimbabwe and Zambia). Gower died in 1860, seven years after Rhodes was born.

383. This is a poetic form of the word "drought."

His story of the battle of Queenston Heights, although in some respect according to history, is much exaggerated, when detailing his own personal achievement in the battle. He said General Brock had expected the Americans to land below Queenston, and sent reinforcements down to prevent them landing. But in the meantime they had landed above, and gained the heights. To retrieve what he had lost was now the objective point in the battle. Brock leading the York volunteers and militia cheering them on with "Have at them now my brave fellows. Well done York volunteers." And observing Philip charging the enemy with extraordinary effect, he shouted "Bravo Gower, you're a hero. We'll gain the day.[384]" At this critical moment Brock fell mortally wounded. Philip raised the fallen General in his arms, he opened his eyes and faintly whispered "You're[385] a brave fellow, Gower; you won the battle."

"Colonel Macdonnell[386] led us on again towards a mass [of] Americans, still unbroken, and the brave fellow fell dead in a few minutes after the gallant Brock. We drove a thousand of them over the heights into the river, as many were made prisoners." So ended the battle of Queenston Heights as told by Philip.

The Battle of Queenston Heights was fought on the 13th[387] of October 1812. It was memorable in the Campaign of that year, and during the whole war, inasmuch as it was won by a few companies of York volunteers and militia with a hundred Indians **[125]** under Joseph Brant, the celebrated Mohawk Chief over a superior force, commanded by an American General of repute, Van Rensselaer.[388] The York Militia and volunteers were lately drawn from pioneer work on their farms. Many of them had been citizens of the United States a few years previous.

Philip served also in the Campaign of 1812 and I think from what I have otherwise heard and read of the taking of York, his story is quite reliable. It is well known that, in battles, and sieges, there are[389] in individual acts of heroism, that are[390] never told in history, also acts of pusillanimity[391] that are only known to a few comrades, and make no part in the history of a battle. A private soldier knows little about evolutions of the enemy or

384. See Back Stories in this chapter.

385. AB "your."

386. Scottish-born Colonel John MacDonnell (1785–1812) was shot off his horse and then shot in the head shortly after Brock's death, dying the next day (October 14). He was memorialized in the Stan Rogers folk song "MacDonnell on the Heights."

387. AB "30th."

388. AB "Ranselar." Stephen Van Rensselaer (1764–1839) was a rich Dutch landowner/aristocrat whose military career ended with the defeat at Queenston Heights.

389. AB "is."

390. AB "is."

391. Pusillanimity refers to cowardliness, lack of courage or resolution.

the manoeuvring[392] of his own corps, or regiment, only what might happen, immediately around himself. Now when you read in Canadian history about the Americans taking York, you will find there is no detail, simply a few facts. Individual losses and suffering are inconsequent to the historian.

Alex and His Mother Stay at the Harleys' Bar

I have mentioned my visit to Toronto in 1839. We went one day, and came home the next afternoon, and night, after disposing of our heterogen[e]ous load. In consequence of this we lodged all night in the Town. The tavern we stayed in was the Brothers' Hotel, or Harley's. It was on the east side of the street from the market,[393] only one building between it and Front Street. The kitchen was in the cellar, and in some way unknown to me now, during the evening, Mother and I found ourselves in the Kitchen listening with great interest to old lady Harley's denunciation of the Americans for demolishing, and pilfering every[th]ing they had. Much of her story was inaud[i]ble to me, but I learned that Harley[394] was a Scotsman of wonderful ability and goodness too generous to live long in this world of sin and misery. Whatever might have been Mr. Harley's goodness [126] in regard to piety, or morality, he certainly did not endow his sons, who in the gift of profanity, refused to be beat in the City of Toronto. It was not the ordinary verbal oaths they swore. They had studied the thing scientifically, Jim Harley while he was alive, was considered the smartest[395] bar keeper in Toronto, and his blasphemy of so sublime a style, that, to strangers, for short time, it was difficult to know whether he was praying or execrating.[396] The Brothers' Hotel was not in any sense an ideal, public house in appearance, to look at outside, and its inside equipment was no better. It was a mystery to many that put up there, what was the attraction towards that one place. It was handy for the market, and [had] a good large yard, and the stables though old and somewhat dilapidated, yet, were comfortable enough. The Harleys knew that a good Hostler was a prime factor in gaining and keeping the public favour. Some fifty years ago, or over James Harley handed in his checks and bade adieu to barroom, liquors, of all kinds, and his courtly oaths, and went where no one ever returns [from]. After Jim's death the

---

392. AB "manureuvering."

393. It was known then as "New Street," and later as "Nelson Street." By the 1880s it was part of Jarvis Street.

394. In the directory of 1837, he was listed as "Harley, John William IV, tavern, New-st, Market Sq." (www.statictorontopubliclibrary.ca/da/pdfs/706129.pdf and Robertson, J. Ross, 1974: 162. There was a William Harley who for a while was part of Captain Cameron's Company of the Regiment of York Militia during the War of 1812-3 (my.tbaytel.net/bmartin/militia.htm.).

395. AB "smartist."

396. AB "execration." To execrate means to swear or express great loathing.

tavern was rented to one Stroud. We continued to put up at his place as long as Stroud kept the house. It was only a short time after Stroud's leaving when fire destroyed all or nearly all the short street between King and Front Street.[397] Before I left the County forty one years ago, the street was built up with spacious buildings. What became of the Harleys or their property I never heard. The boys and girls of this generation of rural York County when they go to Town, and walk down from King Street to Front Street, have no idea of the Harley days. Few alive today used to put up at the old Hotel seventy years ago.

The Battle of York

But to resume Philip's story. On April 27th 1813 nin[e]ty six years ago last April, the Americans under General Pike,[398] landed from their ships oppose the old garrison, as that was the best landing place though [127] a good way west of the Town proper.

Gower's Narrative

"They had five thousand men, we had about three hundred British grenadiers, fine fellows they were, a few Companies of York volunteers and militia. A number of the Americans were Kentucky riflemen, dressed in white frocks[399], blue pants and very wide brim[m]ed hats. They commenced shooting at us as they leaped in the water from their boats. In a few minutes they had formed on the beach, and firing at least three shots four our two. Our bullets did not seem to reach them, while our men fell fast. We could not stand it very long. Our dependence was on the charge of the grenadiers. A mine had been hastily prepared to blow up the Americans when they came to a place where they were closely massed together. Immediately on the springing of the mine the grenadiers were to charge the disordered Americans. But someone had blund[e]red, before the grenadiers were in proper position to charge, the mine blew up, killing more than half of them and only a few of the enemy.[400] This calamity decided the fate of the battle. We ran away to the east of the Town, towards where Gooder[h]am's Mill[401] used to be or perhaps [is] there still. A few of us were

---

397. This was in the Great Fire of 1849, which also involved the burning down of St. James Cathedral.

398. See Back Stories in this chapter.

399. The reference here is to jackets with tails, not to dresses.

400. This is an exaggeration. See Back Stories in this chapter.

401. In 1831, James Worts (c. 1793–1834) established a grist mill. This was taken over by his brother-in-law William Gooderham and his son James Worts after his death. In 1837 a distillery was established there, which remained in operation until closed in 1990. In 2001 the buildings in the area were refurbished and a pedestrian-only arts and entertainment area was established, known as the Distillery District.

rallied and sent to burn a couple of war ships anchored in the eastern part of the bay. The vessels had been hurriedly built of green timber, and we had a terrible job to get the fire agoing. Don't think the Americans wanted to take the ships or they could easily have done so. One of their ships however dropped down and took us prisoners. Gave us a san[d]wich, two biscuits and a slice of raw fat pork between. I tell you it was just as good as 'slick go down'[402] for we were very hungry having tasted nothing since early morning. They only kept us a short time and sent us ashore. The American Militia were still sacking the Town. One fellow had a fie large kettle raised to his shoulder and was going to bring it down with all his might on a large potash kettle. I holl[e]r[e]d "Give that to me," and he threw **[128]** it towards me. As we passed along to join our company where we left them we observed they had smashed everything they did not care to take with them."

The same pot or kettle I have often seen. It was famous in the thirties and forties for stewing apples, cooking potpies, dowdies and pum[p]kins for pies. It was borrowed around the neighborhood to cook the above named dainties, and many more that have[403] slipped my memory, at raisings, logging bees, and weddings. What kind of metal it was composed of or what gave it the renowned excellence in cooking certain kinds of food, I do not think was ever decidedly settled, though often discussed. The people in our locality were content to take its merits for granted, without entering into an analysis of its composition. It was enough for the ladies of that era to known the fact without the aid of science, that it was not ordinary pot, for as they said it was as smooth inside as a porcelain vase.

But to return to Philip and his comrades joining their company. Found some of them lurking in the same place where they left them when taken to burn the ships. There was a piece of chopping to the north of the Kingston road about as far east as the cattle sheds, a little east of Gooder[h]ams. Here a number of Philip's company had hidden from the American scouts who had been around to ascertain if reinforcements were[404] being collected to attack them in a disordered state before getting aboard their ships again.

Back Stories of Chapter Fifteen

Isaac Brock

Isaac Brock (1769–1812) was born in Guernsey, one of the Channel Islands. He is highly respected in Canadian history, for the creative way in which he successfully captured Detroit and for his brave death at the Battle of Queenston Heights on October 13, 1812. The military leaders of

---

402. This was an expression from the southern United States.
403. AB "has."
404. AB "was."

the British/Canadian forces never came close to living up to his reputation or to his skill. He was early nicknamed "the hero of Upper Canada." Even though he was not Canadian, he has long been considered one of the greatest Canadian military heroes, and one of the few that Canadians can name. Brock University in St. Catharines and the city of Brockville in eastern Ontario are both named after him.

Brock's Last Words

An article on a *Military History Now* website with the heading of "Famous last words: the dying utterances of the 11 military commanders" begins with the words: "Whether they are fact or fiction, last words such as these are the stuff of legend in the annals of military history" (www.militaryhistorynow.com/2-14/07/21/famous-last-words-the-dying-utterances-of-11-military-commanders).

They are more than that. A military leader's "last words" reputedly said in dying in battle make up an important narrative in the history of a people. For these leaders were meant to inspire generations to come in warfare.

The story of Isaac Brock's last words made that list. Strangely not included were the famous last words of Captain James Lawrence, U.S. naval officer in the same war, who said "Don't give up the ship."

The actual last words of Major-General Isaac Brock as he was dying from a fatal bullet wound to the chest incurred as he bravely and foolishly led the charge up Queenston Heights on October 13, 1812, are a matter of some speculation. In Robert Malcomson's definitive *A Very Brilliant Affair: The Battle of Queenston Heights, 1812* (2003), Appendix A, pages 231–33, is dedicated to that speculation.

The most often quoted line is "Push on the brave York volunteers" (Malcomson 2003: 147, 231). Ensign John Smith, writing later to Brock's replacement, Lieutenant-Colonel Henry Procter, believed it was "Never mind me, my boys push on," and a local paper had the phrases reversed (Malcomson 2003: 232). Not mentioned by Malcomson is the Brock University tradition that he said "Surgite," which is "press on" in Latin, the motto of the university. George Jarvis, a 15-year-old "gentleman volunteer" claimed that he was close enough to say to the dying Brock, "Are you much hurt, sir?" to which he received no reply but silence (Malcomson 2003: 153).

It is in this context that we can best understand York Militia volunteer Philip Gower's claim to have been praised by Brock. He probably heard about the alleged last words, "Push on the brave York volunteers," and embellished it as an old man to include mention of his personal bravery.

The Battle of York

The Battle of York involved a larger armed force of Americans, around

4,700 men, led by young General Zebulon Pike (1779–1813) against the Major-General Roger Hale Sheaffe (1763–1851), then Lieutenant-Governor of Upper Canada, with about 300 regular, 300 militia (such as Philip Gower), as well as roughly 100 Anishinaabe (I believe including Chief Yellowhead). Outnumbered and strategically out-thought, the Canadian and British forces lost fairly quickly. Sheaffe, who had been awarded a barontcy for his very cautious actions at the Battle of Queenston Heights after Brock's death, and who beat a hasty retreat in this fight, abandoning York for Kingston, where there were armed British vessels, is not mentioned in either battle by Uncle Alex as he, like me, could probably find nothing positive to say about him. He was relieved of his command shortly after his retreat to Kingston.

The number of casualties on the British/Canadian side is hard to measure, as the commander was not around where and when militia, other civilians and Anishinaabe died. It is reasonable to say that neither side had more than 100 die. Pike died in the usually best remembered part of the battle, when a portable magazine (chest of cartridges) exploded not far from where Pike and his men were.

Harley's Tavern

In the Toronto directory of 1837, he was listed as "Harley, John William IV, tavern, New-st, Market Sq." (www.statictorontopubliclibrary.ca/da/pdfs/706129.pdf and Robertson, J. Ross, 1974: 136. Interestingly, in that same directory (Robertson 1974: 162) there was listed "Haverty, Thos. Gentleman, Harley's Tavern." In the directory of 1846–7, there was listed "Harley, John, Brothers' Hotel, 3 east side of Market square."

Chapter Sixteen
Mr. Button, the Clubines, Philip Gower and the Grenadiers' Grave

Mr. Button

A Mr. Button, who in years to come, became somewhat conspicuous in the Township of Markham in raising a Troop of Cavalry known as Button's Troop. These horsemen I have seen on parade. Was intimately acquainted with several members of the troop and while yet a lad I was almost persuaded to joining them, but the want of a horse, a spare horse, was in the way. At a wood bee one winter **[129]** at Mr Benjamin Bowman's,[405] I was dressed up in the uniform of Jim Bowman, he being one of the troop. The uniform was rather becoming, light blue pants and jacket, white or as some called it silver facings, jaunty little cap, and yellow leather sabre belt. The sabre was such I presume was used by light horsemen in the British regiments.[406]

I do not think Mr. Button was an officer in 1813.[407] He had crawled into a hollow log to evade being made prisoner, but whether it was a natural instinct of Mr Button's, peculiar to a large bird of South Africa,[408] that when the head is hidden there is no danger or whether it was simply a miscalculation of his lineal measure, was never known. As a matter of course Mr. Button did not express himself definitely on the subject. At all events his boots were seen protruding from the end of the log by an American, who in words and deed by no means complimentary to the embryo Major, jerked him out of the log much to the amusement of those who witnessed the incident and to the chagrin of Mr. Button. Whether this episode in the military career of the Major had anything to do with the valour of him and his troop was never expressed publicly, but all quietly in the common vernacular of Markham on a training day, such innuendos were[409] quite common in the crowd as:

"Would not amount to much in a battle. Can make a little fuss, an fun in a farmer's field on 24th of May to amuse the boys and girls, that's about all they are good for."

405. He appears to be no relative of Charles Bowman, after whom the town of Bowmanville was eventually named.

406. AB "regiements."

407. See Back Stories in this chapter for a statement to the contrary.

408. It is not true that ostriches stick their heads in the sand to hide from predators. They do crouch down low, necks along the sand, with their feathers presenting decent camouflage. It should also be kept in mind that with their powerful legs they can deliver a killing kick against a predator (www.onekind.org/education/animals_a_ostrich).

409. AB "was."

I believe the young men composing the troop were a fair specimen of the young yeomanry of the County, at that time, and I can see no reason why they could not fight if need be, just as well as their fathers had in 1812 and [']13. Whether it was that they had never been in active service, or whether the people had not faith in the Major's prowess in a battle, or his military **[130]** genius to manoeuvre[410] them properly was consider not of that attainment to bring honour and renown in the County. I cannot tell, but both him and his troop were rather unpopular. I do not think their mounts were of a breed or style suitable for cavalry purposes. A horse that is one half or one quarter heavy draft, that has pulled the plough and harrows all spring could scarcely be supposed to shine as a gallant charger on the Queen's birth day. Or it might be for all I know that his hollow log experience was against him as a true British soldier. Many a jibe and jeer was launched at them. It was aver[r]ed that in attempting a sham charge one of them in brandishing his sabre as if hewing down the foe it fell from his hand, as he galloped on, it was picked up by a big Yorkshire man, who swung it around his head, and swore it was more like a tailor's bodkin than a <u>Surd</u>.[411]

During the winter of 1838 a rumour ran around the County that in the Township of Uxbridge there were[412] a number of rebels hidden in a dense swamp. Major Button and his troop went out to dislodge them, and capture as many prisoners as possible. By a preconcerted[413] understanding between the parties in the swamp, their wives and sympathizers in the neighborhood, that in case of any force coming to storm the swamp, the women for miles around would blow their horns, a custom then to call men away in the woods or fields to their meals, now almost obsolete. It was said the major and his troop did go out to Uxbridge and made a detour, or at least tried to make the detour. When a horn sang out loud and shrill making the welkin[414] ring with its volume of sound. In an instant a hundred horns caused a weird state of mind in the Major and his troop. They expected an ambush, or some devilish cantrip[415] by the rebels, they spurred their horses and galloped off without seeing a rebel. I do not **[131]** vouch for the truth of this story, only that it was current in both Townships during winter.

I have heard it said that there was nothing in a name, that one name was just as good as another, that had Nelson's name been Fiddlesticks, in-

---

410. AB "manuoevre."

411. "Sword" with a presumed Yorkshire accent.

412. AB "was."

413. The word "preconceived" might have been what Uncle Alex wanted to write here.

414. Welkin is an old Germanic word in English that refers to the upper sky. The expression "make the welkin ring" is old in the language, and refers to making a very loud noise.

415. A cantrip is a mischievous or playful trick.

stead of Nelson, he would have been the Hero he was all the same. Had Major Button led[416] his troop on to victory, like Wolf[e] or Brock he would have been glorified with a monument notwithstanding the effeminate name of Button. This may be quite true, with the name of Button, as with many other names. But in all my reading of different types of literature from the dawn of history, down to the present time I have never heard or read of a Button rising very high in the gamut of fame. Two men are associated in my mind with the name of Button. The Major and Bill Button the Tailor,[417] who was a conspicuous character in Cook's Circus,[418] seventy five years ago.

The Clubines

Mr Ezra Clubine, a worthy man of the Township of Whitchurch, and well known by his neighbors, thought to escape captivity from the Americans by hiding in a brush heap. Whether Ezra failed from the same cause as the Major, Philip did not say, but the Yankee that found him threatened to set fire to the heap if he did not evacuate in quick time. The Clubbies were a peculiar people but nowise jealous of good works. Ezra once owned four hundred acres of good land and a Saw Mill on the fourth concession of the Township above named. Ezra was a man of fair mental capacity, and rather intelligent, but he had a propinquity[419] towards going to law, with neighbors and he generally came out of the small end of the horn. His father was one of the pioneer settlers in North York, in the Quaker settlement. As a people they became, or seemed to become phenomenally wealthy. In cases of this kind people who do not know the real cause of prosperity often **[132]** reason that something is wrong, and attribute the getting of the wealth to deeds not in conformity with the precepts taught in the ten commandments. It was alleged by the neighborhood of the Clubine family, that a pedlar was known to go to their house, ostensibly for the purpose of lodging for the night. The Pedlar was never seen again, but the young Clubbies were seen with han[d]kerchiefs and braces, and other paraphernalia generally carried by pedlars. There was an old well on the Clubine farm and neighbors aver[r]ed that at certain times the airy form of a pedlar was seen flitting around this old well. The well was known to be filled up immediately after the disappearance of the pedlar. On a certain night each year, as long as the Clubine family lived on the arm, all the stumps on the farm seemed to be on fire, but in the morning the stumps remained unburned. This tale of the Clubine family, and their sudden acquisition of

416. AB "lead."

417. See Back Stories in this chapter.

418. There was a Cook's Circus in Edinburgh during Uncle Alex's time. Perhaps as a travelling show it might have made its way to Aberdeen during his childhood.

419. He probably meant to write "propensity."

wealth, is perhaps about one century old, and has passed out of memory to all Whitchurch people except a very few who, now must be on the borders of four score years, and with years has passed away to oblivion the very name of Clubine for all I know.[420]

The Grenadiers' Grave

[Philip Gower's Narrative]

After the departure of the American army in the evening, we retired up Town and towards the scene of the conflict. Next day came the burying of the dead. The Volunteers and the Militia who had fallen[421] were mostly taken home and buried by their own people. The wounded were cared for in York in a kind of improvised hospital. The Americans carried away their dead and wounded. For the unfortunate grenadiers we dug a trench about ten feet wide and five feet deep, laid them side by side rolled in their blankets. We felt more sorrow for the grenadiers, then for our own men, for we had a chance to run away, they were the victims of a blunder.[422]

In 1835, after the lapse of twenty two years, this last resting place of many a one who was once a mother's pride and a father's hope and joy was point[ed] out as the grenadiers' grave. Seventy one years ago, when I saw it, there was nothing to be seen in memory of the gallant men whose lives were ignobly sacrificed by a blunder but a slight depression on the plain.

It was a quiet afternoon in June, that a few young lads and myself visited this historic spot in the Annals of Toronto. A dozen or more men and women were standing around this lonely grave sacred to at least to two companies of the flower of British Soldiers. Some of these men and women had been residents of York at the time of the ill fated blunder. They believed that had this mistake had not been made, the Americans would have been defeated and the Town saved from being pillaged. These men with sorrow depicted on their faces lifted their hats in honour to the dead. Women turned aside weeping.[423]

For all I know, this hallowed grave is now forgotten, and built over with houses. Not over one year ago I read of some excavations being made for some purpose in the neighborhood of the Old [G]arrison, and a number of human bones being among the debris. It was mentioned at the time in the

---

420. Sarah or Sally Gower was the first wife of Israel Clubine. They married around 1843 and had at least seven children.
421. AB "falled."
422. Gower was referencing the exploding magazine here.
423. AB "weaping."

Globe the bones were relics of the unfortunate grenadiers.[424]

There are[425] a few incidents of early times and manners of the people I may allude to later[426] on, not of much interest to the present generation but to illustrate customs and opinions now in Old Ontario almost obsolete. In regard to family ancestry[427] I can add little appertaining directly to our family. But notice in reading over the narrative that I have omit[t]ed to give any biographic sketch of certain of the families mentioned. In the meantime I will draw this [134] part of my narrative to a close with a brief panegyric on old Philip.

His character was formed by the circumstances and influences brought to bear on his mind in the age and society in which he lived. He had received no education in the common acceptance[428] of the word, or any religious instructions, at least in his younger days. His perceptions of right and wrong were intuitive, and impulsive, without much regard to reason. His actions were often guided[429] by low cunning. His practical knowledge of his surroundings in which necessity often became paramount was unfailing. He knew the country from Dundas to Whitby, he knew the country from Lake Ontario to Lake Simcoe, and from Whitby north to Lake Scugog. He was a trapper of the olden time. To use poison to kill foxes, wolves and minks he regarded as little better than fratricide, even the use of scent to entice a creature into a trap as a most ungenerous act. His principle was 'my knowledge <u>agin</u> brute cunning, if the brute knows too much for let him live.' His mind from youth up was almost wholly influenced by the principle common among Americans of his class, who came into the world immediately after the revolution. But although tinged with the wrong doings and wrong sayings of the times, he would often rise above the spirit of the times in which he had been nurtured, and gave evidence of excellent sense, generosity and executive ability. No one could be kinder or more willing to give help in time of need. At times when his individuality was aroused, as in the case of the Indian scare, he could at the Captain and Counsellor, indicating that had he been blessed with a common education and social surroundings of an intelligent community, he might have been conspicuous as one of the leading men of his class.

In regard to his religious belief he was very reticent. He did [135] make some profession once at a Camp Meeting, because he understood they were Rebel Methodists. He attended the protracted meetings for a while.

---

424. See Back Stories in this chapter.

425. AB "is."

426. AB "latter."

427. AB "ancestory."

428. AB "acception."

429. AB "guarded."

But as the old sayings are often fraught with much truth, "What is bred in the bone, is hard to take out of the flesh". Philip thought no harm in setting fire to stumps on his way for the cows on a Sabbath evening. To haul in hay or grain on Sunday if it was fit during a wet season. This was all right in his theology. Trying how the trout would bite on a Sunday afternoon was regarded by him as quite legitimate, notwithstanding his experience in the praying circle of the Rebel Methodists. But these traits of character were not confined to Philip alone. His class of men in the church and outside the church were apt to have a little shooting match away in the backfield or woods on a Sunday afternoon, and if it had not been for fear of the law, Sunday shooting would have been quite common.[430] They thought no harm of it. One who has been accustomed to blaspheme from the time he could lisp the first words, perhaps an oath, fiends a difficulty in being always on guard, in expression. In conversation one day with a Methodist Exhorter, Philip asked him if Brown was on the circuit now. "Yes" was the reply, "Bya <u>Gad</u> I would not like to be him." Whether his knowledge of the plan of salvation as sufficient for his redemption, the All Righteous Judge will draw the line in the right place. It might be when the great day of Judgement comes, and the just as separated[431] from the unjust, that some who knew Philip in this life, and believed their assurance of eternal bliss to be a foregone conclusion and pitied Phillips chance of salvation may be mistaken. Although this old pioneer gave few evidences of being born again, who knows but in the secret chamber of his heart, he had a passport to Heaven. [136]

The type of men to which Philip belonged have passed away and will never return again on this earthen ball of ours. How well they served their day and generation is portrayed on rural and urban Ontario. They fought the forest primeval, they suffered the turmoil and privations attendant to all who are the first to go into the wilderness and make homes for themselves and future generations.

Had the early pioneers of the County of York during the first part of the nin[e]teenth century, had the least idea that what in the near future was to be, they would have been more alert in securing property that became of great value before they died. They never dreamed that muddy little York was to become the Metropolis it now is of the Banner Province of the Dominion. Philip Gower could have had one hundred acres of land where the old jail[432] stood in 1835, now the heart of the City, but would not have it

---

430. The Upper Canada Lord's Day Act of 1845 prohibited shooting, fishing, hunting and the playing of sports such as golf or tennis on a Sunday. Uncle Alex obviously was raised with a strict Scottish sense of Sabbatarianism, feeling that Sunday should be kept holy by not being involved with anything considered "frivolous."

431. AB "seperated" here and elsewhere.

432. This was on King Street not far from the St. Lawrence Market.

in a gift, so uncompromising was the quality of the land and the situation.

The site of Toronto and a[d]jacent part of the County was no choice farming land. When men had a whole Province to select from they were very fastidious, and as various in their choice as the desires of the different individuals. Hence settlements were mad[e] away back, in land, wherever good hard wood land prevailed, leaving indifferent soil behind, looking no further ahead than immediate necessity. In 1835 the Ridges of Whitchurch (except here and there on the south side of the ridge) was a dense forest of excellent white pine and red oak. On the south and north border of the ridge some very fair farms were taken up. Otherwise the land was very light. So exceedingly light in many places that I have stuck my walking stick down to the end with simply the pressure of one hand. This land was considered no good by the early settlers, would not grow white [**137**] leaves was the common expression, still it became valuable before the death of many of those early settlers that passed it by. Many miles away to the northeast stretched a large trace of land yet the undisturbed abode of the bear, wolf and deer. While away north as far as Barrie, Orillia, Beaverton, Penetanguishene and Coldwater—settlements had been made. The changes in my time seem too great to grasp. The fact that I have seen pine stumps on Queen street in 1835 seems in 1906 to be apocryphal.

The hero of the latter part of my story rests in peace in the little graveyard by the Baptist Church on the Townline between Markham and Whitchurch, by this time forgotten.[433]

Thomas Gray
"Elegy Written in a Country Churchyard" – Stanzas 11 and 12

Can storied urn or animated bust
Back to its mansion call the fleeting breath
Can honour's voice provoke the silent dust
Or flattery sooth[e] the dull cold ear of death
Perhaps in this neglect spot is laid
Some heart once pregnant with celestial fire
Hands that an empire might have swayed[434]
Or waked to ecstasy[435] the living lyre

===================

433. See Back Stories in this chapter.
434. "Hands that a rod of empire might have swayed."
435. AB "exctacy."

John Steckley
"Mortality" by William Knox (1789–1825), second stanza

The leaves of the oak and the willow shall fade
Be scattered around and together be laid
And [the] young and the old and the low and the high
Shall moulder to dust and together shall lie
Three stones, with their heads of moss,
A tree with scarce a leaf.
Long grass that whistles in the wind.
Is all that [138] marks the place of the mighty Monar [?]
With three steps I encompass thy grave
Oh he who was so great before

Even this humble tribute has been denied to [the] humble hero of Queenston Heights.

When quite a young man, like many other young men, I tried my hand at verse making. I knew well I was no <u>Rhymer</u> and could have told what I had to tell better in my prose. But I was told he was an excellent subject for a beginner. So here it is from memory a kind of dirge to Philip when afflicted by one of his aberrant spells[.]

====================

When proud ambition kindles strife
And nations madly rise
They do not value loss of life
Nor wives nor orphans cries
Many fight for honour's sake
To gain a mighty name
And others fight but to arouse
Vile passion's fire to flame
There's some whose valiant actions are
Unseen midst war's alarms
Ignobly bleed on fields afar
From home and all its charms
Such was the case with Philip Gower
He'd been in many fights
He fought at York <u>gainst</u> Yankee power
And charged up Queenston's Heights
And many a deadly rifle ball
Came whistling past his ear [139]
His comrades round him fast did fall
 But Philip knew no fear

With musket good and bayonet fixed
He fired and charged anon
When many a comrade brave had fallen
Midst battle's din and throng
Long and loud the cannons pealed
There direful notes of woe
And many a Yankee's fate was sealed
On Queenston Heights laid low
But Philip stood and bravely fought
When many a man had fallen
And General Brock rode past and called
A hero brave I'll warrant
A word in season oft has changed
The fate of battle grim
Such was the case in Queenston's Heights
When Brock and Philip joined
The battle won but now alas
The gallant fell wounded
And Philip wrapped him in his cloak
And wept where he expired
A monument on Queenston's Heights
For valiant Brock was raised
In memory of his gallant deeds
But Philip nee'r was praised
And now a raving maniac he
Does wander night and day [**140**]
He cares not for his home nor friends
His reason's fled away

====================

Back Stories of Chapter Sixteen

Major John Button

John Button (1770–1861) was born in Connecticut. He and his wife moved to Canada, in the Niagara region, in 1799, and were granted 200 acres of land beside Yonge Street in 1801. The town of Buttonville, named after him, would eventually be established in the area. He joined the militia prior to the War of 1812. He received permission for that war as a Captain to raise a troop of cavalry that became known as the 1st York Light Dragoons. Like Philip Gower, he was forced to surrender at Fort York, taken prisoner on April 27, 1813. As far as I know there is not corroborating evidence concerning Uncle Alex's story about the situation surrounding his capture. It may have just been a rumour in the area at the time. Uncle Alex may have liked the story because he found Major Button to be pompous, and a Tory.

He was raised to Major and kept in command, part time, of the 1st York Light Dragoons. His son Francis followed him into the troop, as did his grandson, Francis' son, William. His sympathies were with the Tories and against William Lyon Mackenzie, so his troop were prepared to fight against the Rebels. They engaged in no battles. The 1st York Light Dragoons continue to this day, but are known today as part of The Governor General's Horse Guard.

Billy Button the Tailor

Billy Button the Tailor is a traditional comic figure in English history. In July 1768, there debuted an equestrian parody with a clumsy rider named Bill Button the Tailor (as the parody itself was titled). In the music hall song entitled "Easter Monday For Ever, or, the Cobbler of Greenwich," the cobbler character sings the words:

> But when I got home, (it is true, on my life)
> Bill Button the tailor, was off with my wife.
> (George Cruikshank and Robert Cruikshank 1925: 420)

The Grenadiers' Burial

For a good account of burials of victims of the Battle of York see Stephen Otto's fine "Where the Bodies are Buried." Concerning the 1905 find, he reports the following:

> ... in May, 1905, ... a single skeleton ... [was found] by some officers inspecting some trench-digging near the lake midway between Strachan Avenue and Stanley Barracks. The find was made at a depth of about two feet; two short pipes and one corroded brass button had accompanied the soldier to his grave. The newspaper report concluded on a languid note: "It is believed that there were other bodies buried about the spot, but that the lake had washed that part of the land away (Otto 2006: 1).

Philip Gower

Philip Gower (1781–1860) was buried in the Dickson Hill Cemetery in Markham, along with his wife Mary Sarah Fockler Gower (1791–1844), who shares his gravestone. In that cemetery as well are their daughters Catherine Gower Schell (1815–1858) and Sarah Gower Clubine (1820–

1859). Philip Gower (1811–1891) left the area for the United States, where he was buried apart from the rest of the family.

Chapter 17
Return to Family

His Father's Sisters and Their Families

In telling what I have heard, and what I know of my forebears and relations, I slipped by some families without any comment. I shall now endeavour to tell you something of them.

I had already told you of my father's four brothers, and six Sisters. They were all alive when we left Scotland. I am not sure of the order of birth. I think however that Mr[s] John Grant (Annie) was the eldest in the family. Her husband imported lime from somewhere, came in small ships, he had a yard and shed to keep it in. Supplied not only the Town, but farmers took cart loads of it to put on their land. He was a man of few words, but staunch in principle. They had five sons and two daughters. Jimmie the eldest son was sailing with the *Dwina*, first in the Quebec lumber trade, then in the Baltic trade but subsequently became Mate of an East Indiaman and died at Calcutta, never heard what became of his family. George continued in the Greenland whale fishing, as long as the ship the *Joseph Green* remained in the whaling trade.[436] Think from what I have heard, he left his ship at San Francisco the time of the gold fever. Told his mother that he walked across the continent of America, from the Pacific to the Atlantic, that he went into a house (a farm house) to get a night's lodgings and it turned out to be his Uncle's house. Of course this was a sailor's yarn but his mother believed him. We never saw the fellow. As long as our Uncle Jamie sailed from Hamburg, Jack sailed with him. Jack I think was [an ap]prentice in the *Dwina*, and on the voyage had some words with the mate, a fight ensued, and the Mate came out second best. When the ship arrived at Quebec Jack skipped, and never went back to Peterhead and [**141**] we lost track of him. Sandie the fourth son was sailing thirty years ago. William the youngest son was still in Peterhead and foll[ow]ing his father's business, the last we heard of him. Mary the eldest daughter was married to a blacksmith Thomas Henderson before we left PHD. The youngest girl Jean married a brother to Mary's husband both living in Aberdeen the last we heard of them.

I think the next oldest in my father's family was Elizabeth or as we knew her Auntie Lizzie. She was a widow, had one daughter known to us as Bell Mill or Milne, have been at her house, remember her quite well. Think she liked a draw of her pipe occasionally. When she came to Town she generally smoked [?] in a new pipe or two. Jean or Mrs Robertson also a widow, lived in the village of St. Fergus, kept a school [for] the Village children. She had two sons, Jamie and Sandie, James when quite a young

---

436. The *Joseph Green* of Peterhead went whaling under Captain James Volum in 1842 (Campey 2002: 76)

lad listed into the 78 Highlanders and away to Indian before I was born. The regiment went to Ceylon, stationed as Trincomalee, remember letters coming from him to my father, think I have one of his letters in my possession. After being in India fourteen years they came home to recruit. He went out to St. Fergus to see his mother, he mentions that the guard of the coach [?] sang the 'Sogers Return' which caused the tears to run down his cheeks, as scenes of his boyhood came to view. After recruiting in Aberdeen the regiment[437] moved to England. Just before leaving Aberdeen to go to England or immediately on arriving at a Town called Colne, my father received a letter from him stating that war had broken out in Afghanistan[438] and it was rumoured in military circles the 78th would go to India again, and a letter addressed to Pay Master Sergeant James Robertson 78th Highlander Colne England or elsewhere would find him. My father answered this letter. They went to Afghanistan. The 78th were nearly annihilated.[439] We never heard of him again. He told in some of his letters he was married to a girl of the regiment and had family but what became of them we never heard.

Sandie Robertson learned the trade of cart and plough wright, had a shop in the village and doing a good business. He must be dead for he was a young man seventy one years ago. Never heard anything about his family.

Aunt Mary or Mrs Center had a large family. Her husband was a very clever man and all the family appeared to partake of his mental capacity. One of his sons, John, came to the United States and took up land in Wisconsin. In 1843 the family all except one son came to Wisconsin. Uncle Alexander Center and Aunt Mary came up country from Quebec, as they sailed from Aberdeen to Quebec, they came to Toronto and came out to see us, stayed about a week. They brought a daughter with them, a most amiable girl—in one week she had gained our hearts that we cried a whole day when she went away. We heard from them several times, but when the old people died correspondence ceased.

Aunty Bell or Mrs Mitchell lived in the Village of New Dean, have seen them think Mr Mitchell was a shoemaker. Never saw any of their family.

I am not sure which was the eldest, Bell or Meggy. Meggy was Mrs. Scott. She was a widow, her husband was killed from going down in a well he was digging, by foul air or carbonic acid gas. Have seen one son who came to this country and settled somewhere in the neighborhood of Owen Sound, think some of his sons are there at present. Now I have gone over all the Aunts, as far as my memory serves me.

437. AB "regiement" here and elsewhere.

438. AB "Afaganstan."

439. This took place in 1842 in the first Anglo-Afghan War. The regiment suffered its greatest military losses followed two years later by many deaths due to cholera. Both killed women and children of the regiment as well as the men.

John Steckley
His Father's Brothers and Their Families
The Romances of Cousin John Brodie

Now for the Uncles. Uncle Sandie as we knew him, had a farm or was in a place called the Shiel[440] Hill. Was once at his place. His wife was called Auntie Susie. The oldest boy John better known as Jock, [en]listed into the [**143**] 92nd now called the Gordon Highlanders. He was quite young and they required him home. I remember the father and mother coming to Town sometimes, my father, sometimes my mother, went with them to different parties whose boys had [en]listed, and were bought off, to get advice. After a good deal of trouble of trouble, they succeeded in getting him off 20 or 25 pound sterling. He was not at home a year when a recruiting party came around again. The sergeant was heard saying "We'll get him again." And they did get him. Of course they did not attempt to b[u]y him off the second time. When we left Peterhead he was in Gibraltar with the regiment. He had a girl in Scotland, had plighted hands and faith to be true to each other. John was favoured by the Colonel in fact acted as his guard and body servant. He got leave from the Colonel to come home and marry his girl. A private soldier getting this privilege from the Colonel, the woman belongs to the regiment, and is taken wherever they go, and children, if any, are educated, and cared for by the regiment, or rather the Government. John came home to his father's and told what he came for, the family said nothing for, or against the marriage but knew well there could be no marriage at this time. John was told where he would find the girl. He went straight to the house, and knocked at the door, it was opened by John's girl and a baby in her arms. She was married. For one brief instant eyes spoke louder than words. She hung her head and John wheeled around and sped back to Gibraltar as fast as time and conveyance could carry him. The same routine in the regiment went on as previous to John's wedding escapade, he continued to carry messages for the Colonel to, and from the Spanish Town of Gibraltar, which is old being important when the Moors held Andalusia.[441] Many of the streets have balconies[442] reaching out almost to the middle of the street. On these balconies in the summer evenings [**144**] were[443] the rendezvous, coquetry and sere[n]adding. In John's walks back and forth to Town, he passed under several balconies. He had observed that a small piece of paper fell from the end of the balcony. For several times he took no notice, but one day in passing a billet[444] fell on his hand, he picked it up and looking up saw a beautiful young lady smiling

---

440. AB "Sheil."

441. Andalusia refers to an area in the south of Spain.

442. AB "balconys" here and elsewhere.

443. AB "was."

444. This refers to a "billet-doux" or a love letter.

down to him. John put the billet-doux, as it turned [out] to be in his pocket and with his cane went through the beautiful motion of presenting arms, which is due alone to officers of high rank in the British army. But John could not read the billet-doux, only knowing a few words of Spanish. The Colonel and his wife could read Spanish fairly well, and for the novelty of the thing became a kind of go between and interpreters. The result was that they young lady was wealthy and gladly produced the twenty pounds to buy him off. And the bonnie sojer became a Don something I have I have forgotten. I have rather abridged this story. It is not near so full nor as pathetic as came from his father.

Alex Falls in Love with Cousin Sarah Brodie

Of the younger members of Uncle Sandie's family I have no recollection whatever, I remember Sarah and Janet, Sarah used to come and stay with us a while in summer. My earliest impressions of her, was washing my feet, putting me to bed, and hearing me say my prayers. She was an excellent singer, and was nowise scrupulous in giving a song when asked. She never had a cold nor any of the excuses good singers often make, until half the enjoyment is sacrificed. She was very fair, and an abundance of golden hair arranged in some mystic way on the crown of her head, and fastened with a large comb. I often sneaked up to the back [of] her chair and pulled out the big comb, and let the rich golden braids flow around her neck. She did not get angry, as a good many girls would do, at a little innocent mischief in a little boy. With her golden **[145]** locks, pink cheeks, and ruby lips, the jaunty head poised on a neck superb in creamy whiteness and her dark blue eyes were clear and bright as sap[p]hires. In short her tout ensemble in my eye was faultless. She was with us one summer, perhaps when I was seven years old. I returned from school as early as possible. I looked for Sarah in the kitchen which was her usual resort, she was not there. Something had happened, the house appeared to be deserted, knew the others boys had not returned from school, thought my mother and the younger children had gone upstairs with Mrs Sellar. At last I took a peep into the room, or parlour when lo and behold, I was struck dumb with what I saw. There was my idol, to me the very incarnation of everything good and lovely witting on a fellow's knee, and as little Bobby[445] said to his mansa[446] Ma, "Ma Jack Walton is in the parlour and he has got sister Sal on his knee, and he's biting her face all over, and she don't cry one bit." The fellow had a rather countrified[447] appearance. I spoke not, I moved not, but steadily gaped at

---

445. Current when Uncle Alex was writing was a series of humourous American books entitled *Caricature: Wit and Humor of a Nation in Picture, Song and Story*. Little Bobby and Jack Walton were regular characters in this series.

446. I am not sure what this word is supposed to be.

447. AB "countrified."

them. They did not see me, or, at least, they were so absorbed in their own affair that they did not care whether I had ever had an existence.[448] I hated the fellow, with a hatred so intense that had I been able I would have done him bodily harm.

Now what kind of love was this that I had for Sarah. Boyish love is often called calf love. Then there is sexual love, and Platonic love. I am inclined to believe my affection for Sarah was not calf love, nor sexual love, but purely Platonic. I had no selfish or sinister motive whatever. I had no cause to hate the man, because he loved her. I had no cause to do him bodily harm, but I could not help it, I did not like him. And what of Sarah's affection for the little boy, was it Platonic or simply a kind of blown on blue[449] **[146]**, let Savants tell. Well after we left Peterhead a year or two Sarah married this fellow.

After my love escapade with Sarah, Janet came to P.H.D. to go to school, and finish her education. She rented a room, in the Society Close and boarded herself. Janet was considered a famous beauty, and she might have been more beautiful than Sarah to connoisseurs in the beauty line but not to me. I was sent many times to her room with a message or a parcel. In my boyish thought I did not think Janet was a very ardent scholar. I sometimes observed a question on her slate, half done, while she was munching away at sweeties. She was very liberal with her sweeties, candy-glue, and Solomon's[450] temple, and never failed to give me liberally. One day she had given me a little more than usual and I had a surplus to take home. Of course I told I got them from Janet. My mother shook her head and "I; I; she's getting ouer monie[451] sweeties. Oer monie lads." She did not continue long at school and I never heard very much about her sequel after we came to this country. Think I have heard she had a daughter or granddaughter married to a farmer north of St. Mary's.

In regard to our Uncle Willie he left his ship at Quebec. Was in the lumbering trade up the Ottawa. In the employ of a Mr Roebuck a lumber merchant company, hear quarters Bytown, now Ottawa. He was alive when we came to this country as one of the raftsmen[452] my mother spoke to onboard the St. George knew him. Father wrote to Bytown several times but received no answer. A Presbyterian Minister from Bytown, Mr Cruickshank my father got acquainted[453] with through the Revd George Galloway of Markham. Mr Cruickshank learned there was such a man well known

---

448. AB "existance."

449. "Blown on blue" is a kind of blue glassware.

450. AB "Soloman's."

451. She seems to be saying "over many."

452. AB "raftsman."

453. AB "acquanted."

among the lumber men but of his whereabouts or his address he could learn nothing. At last word came from Scotland [147] he was dead and had left money and property in Bytown. The people at home were anxious to find out all about it and see how much there would be to each one of the relatives. But nothing could be heard of him or his property from Ottawa. A letter was written to Mr Roebuck then an English member of parliament. It was unanswered or had never reached him. Perhaps was improperly addressed. So ended all knowledge of Uncle Willie. Betty was his daughter but I do not think we ever saw her.

Regarding Uncle Jamie's family, the Captain and the Mosey's, I know very little only when we left Peterhead he was sailing a ship from London to Hamburg.

I have given a short synopsis of the families near of kin as far as I have heard and remember.

After the second generation, kinship begins to get obscure. When correspondence ceases, estrangement soon renders kindred almost obsolete, as far as we know at least.

We have relations in France no further removed than second and third cousins. In Spain, perhaps in India, New Zealand, Australia and numbers in the United States.

BACK STORIES OF CHAPTER SEVENTEEN

George Brodie's Siblings
Sisters
1. Annie Brodie (Mrs. John Grant)
Jimmy   George   Jack   Sandie   William
Mary (Henderson)   Jean (Henderson)

2. Elizabeth (widow)
Bell   Milne

3. Jean (Robertson)
Jamie   Sandie

4. Mary (Mrs. Alexander Center)
John

5. Bell (Isabella; Mrs. Mitchell)

6. Meggy (Margaret; Mrs. Scott)

John Steckley

Brothers
1. Alexander (Sandie) + Susie
   John   Sarah   Janet

2. George

3. William (Willie)
   Betty

4. James (Jamie)

From Chapter One:
Father's Side
Alexander Brodie   Barbara Anderson Brodie
Anne   Jean   Elizabeth   Mary   Margaret   Isabella   Alexander
George   William   James

Chapter Eighteen
A Trip to the St. Lawrence Market

The following truthful story may be interesting for young people of the present day, to at least try and realize the wonderful change from sixty four years ago, to the present day. In April 1842[454] a load of potatoes, fowls, home made cheese, eggs, and a kit of butter was gotten ready in the afternoon, and stowed away in the wagon as well as possibly could be done, considering the size of the box. After much discussion and no little diplomacy. It was at last decided that owing to the sugar making and chopping still to do, Mother and I could best be spared to go to Toronto and dispose of this multifarious products of the farm. Accordingly we left home about midnight. We had [148] [a] middling fair team but too much of a load for the state of the roads. However we got fairly well with breathing the horses oc[c]asionally until we came to Yonge Street, South of Richmond Hill. The frost was quite out and with much travel it was mud almost to the axles.[455] The mud was of so tenacious a nature that it adhered to the wheels between the spokes as made the wheel appear like a circle of mud from felly[456] to hub. About half a mile south of Richmond Hill we stuck fast. After many vain attempts to extricate the wagon, the horses refused to pull I got a rail from the fence, and, getting it under the hub of hone of the fore wheels, I called to the horses while m mother plied[457] the whip. As I lifted until everything was green, and my boot went down in the mud, when attempt[ing to] pull up my foot the boot stayed in the tenacious clay. I used every word and epithet I knew to make them pull. Some of them perhaps not in strict conformity with parliamentary etiquette but all in vain. There was a house on the Markham side of the street[458] about a hundred yards south. The house was up a lane a short distance from Yonge Street. I went up and knocked. A dapper looking young man in long white nightgown opened the door. I told him my condition in as few words as possible, and politely asked him if he would be so kind as help me down to the stone road and I would pay him handsomely for his trouble. He answered me gruffly, he only had a yoke of oxen he was not accustomed [to] driving them and his boys were not at home. I came back to the wagon and reported my entire failure in getting help. We made another effort to get the wagon out. This time I lifted until I saw stars around me, with the same result, the wagon

454. There is some problem with the year, as Nordheimer's store, which he went to in order to buy a fife, opened in 1844.

455. AB "axels."

456. The felly is the rim or the part of the rim into which the spokes of a wheel are inserted.

457. AB "plyed."

458. That would be on the east side.

did not move. My feet sank down in the mud over the top of my boots, when I drew up my feet the boots were left in the mud. This was too much for my equanimity and I cursed the man, horses [149] and road. My mother by this time was crying and beseeching me not to blaspheme it would [do] no good, she would go and entreat the man again. I carried her across the mud to the side of the road. She knocked, he got up and opened the door, but before she told her story, he slam[m]ed the door in her face and turned the key. I assisted her into the wagon again. By this time there was a little daylight and I perceived another house not far from the road. I went to this house and knocked. A little man, like the other man in immaculate night robe opened the door. My heart sank for I had seen enough of white robed men. And from that morning to this day, I have never had on a nightgown on my body. There is no garment worn by the male sex that I hate to see, and abhor so much as this most effeminate looking thing. Well I told him my story, he said,

"I'm very sorry for you young man, but my team are colts and I durst not take them to pull out a load[ed] wagon, the way the roads are now. You know it would spoil them forever. If I had an old team I'd only be too glad to help you young man. I see you've been in hard luck this morning. How old are you."

I told him 16 "and your mother sitting out there in the wagon?" "yes". I was turning away when I heard a pleasant female voice plead "Oh Joseph you might help the boy, and his mother sitting out there in the wagon, by old Keelors, the old hog, his boys are not away." "Simply impossible my dear. Simply impossible. But I'll tell you young man, if you go up this lane to the next house, there's a man up there that I am sure will help you."

I thanked him and walked away up the lane as fast as I could, and came to the house. The family were not up. I rapped at the door and immediately a response came "Helo what wa-ant" "I want some help." "Ah". In a minute [150] the man was at the door. He looked me over, "wa-al sonny thous ban aithe mud." I had struck on a thorough bred Yorkshire man. As soon as I heard the familiar and well known patois I anticipated help. I told him my trouble. "Come Dick geet oop fast as thou can boot harness on tink an doll and help this lad down to the stai-n road." "Wha-at you've gotten load?" I told him I had pink eye potatoes. "All right give Dick wha-at you think right o' pink eyes."

He then went to a cupboard and took a bottle and a cup and poured into the cup two thirds the full of it. "Drink this lad, do you good, you've been a sweaten." I drank it but it was more whisky than I ever drank at once in my life before. He poured out a good draught to himself and another to Dick who had come out with the team. Dick mounted old tink, the man gave me a leg on to doll, he said "marniin lad."

Whether this man is alive or not I will never know, but he befriended me in great distress, and I have never forgotten his kindness. Dick hitched on in front of my team and after some trouble in getting the team to pull together we got the wagon out and down to the stone road.[459] Dick took a bag full of potatoes for his services, said "I wish you safe home again lad."

Well we got into the city at last rather late in the forenoon. I sold my potatoes to an Irishman. He appeared to be a truthful[460] man. Said he lived up Queen Street a piece. I asked him if it was a good stoned street. "Well no but it is well turnpiked."[461] Well I went on, and on, and kept asking him if we were near the place now. His unvariable answer was about forty rods.[462] I arrived at his house at last at least one mile and a half from the market. His wife came to the door and looked at the potatoes, and said "are they[y] good." "Yes" he says. "<u>Auh</u> he says, af course" he says. Now Rogers if them <u>pratties</u>[463] is not [151] good you know how <u>it</u> il be, <u>thir</u> pink eyes, Pink, pink, the divil who ever heard pratties havin pink eyes." From this colloquy between Mr Rogers and his loving spouse it was easy to opine who was the Premier in the Rogers Cabinet.

It was well on to on o'clock before I got back to the market, and got the horses in the stable. My mother had made the most of her purchase, and thought we should be ready as soon as the horses were fed and rested to go home. This was true but the horses had not eaten anything since we left home, but a bit and drink at Finches[464] as we came in. I had an order from a blacksmith to deliver at a hardware store for iron. I had a strong temptation not to deliver the order, as I knew we had load enough with the empty wagon. Reason said do not take the iron, conscience said you promised and the road may be dried up a little. I delivered the order and the man promised to have the iron ready when I came up the street.

When our financial affairs were[465] settled in some way I cannot now explain, there was three York shillings (thirty seven and a half cents) coming to me. I had been very anxious to learn to play on a fife or flute. I had made a kind of fife to myself, by boring a hole in a hard beech stick with a small pod auger, plugging up one end and burning the finger holes with a red hot wire. It was not quite true but would play a tune middling. William McLenan the piper could play very nicely on it. But I was anxious for a

459. The stone road would have started a little south of Thornhill, which would be a few miles down the road (Berchem 1977: 159). I'm guessing that would have it at Steeles Avenue.

460. AB "truthfull."

461. AB "turnpicked." The man appears to be saying that it was improved in some way.

462. As a rod is a bit more than five metres, this would be a little over 200 metres.

463. Pratties is Irish English for potatoes.

464. The Finch family had a small farm and an inn or tavern on the east side of Yonge Street by the east-west street that now bears their name.

465. AB "was."

better one. I went straightway up King Street to Nordheimer's[466] store, and bought a fife, I have that fife to this day.

Back Stories of Chapter Eighteen

Abraham Nordheimer

Abraham Nordheimer (1816–1862) was an early Toronto musician and merchant born to a Jewish family from Bavaria. He went to New York in 1839, then to Kingston in 1842 where he first established a store, and then with his brother Samuel set up the first music store in Toronto in 1844 (A. and S. Nordheimer Co.). They sold musical instruments, and published and sold sheet music, very successfully. Eventually the family would prosper to the extent that they would set up a piano manufacturing company, the oldest such in Canada. It later became a brand name within the Heintzman company. His last name was given to what is now a location for a popular nature walk, Nordheimer's Ravine in downtown Toronto.

466. AB "Nordeheimers."

Chapter Nineteen
The Success and Romancing of Dr. John Walters

If that old fife had the gift, or power of retrospection it could tell many a tale of joy, and also sorrow. Many boys and girls who were in their teens.

[*Piety in Youth*—Rev. Dr. Thomas Blacklock (1721-1791)][467]
When life's gay morn, in when sprightly youth, with vital ardour glows.
And shines and in all the fairest charms, which beauty can disclose.
[152]
Deep on they soul, before its powers are yet vice enslaved,
Be thy Creator's glorious name, and character engraved
For soon the shades of grief shall cloud the sunshine of thy days.
And cares and toils, in endless round encompass all thy ways.
Soon shall thy heart the woes of age, in mournful groans deplore,
And sadly muse on former joys, that now return no more.

Few boys and girls that were in their teens when I was sixteen are on this side the bourn[468] that separates[469] time from eternity. I have heard it said that what has been may come again. That is not my experience. The same causes may produce similar results in so far as the physical world is concerned, but socially seldom.

Bonnie Bessie Lee (1860-1880) – excerpt[470]
But time changes a' things the ill-natured loon[471]
Where it was sae rightfully he'll no let it be
But I rubbit atmy een, and I thought it would swoon.

How the circle had come round about our ain Bessie Lee.[472] So said Robert Nichol[l][473] in a song many years ago. And the truism is the same today as in olden time.

Many a man, and many a woman have changed their mind in a few

---

467. He was a blind Scottish poet

468. Cognate with the Scots term "burn," refers to a a small stream, especially one that flows intermittently or seasonally.

469. AB "seperates."

470. "The Word on the Street, Broadside Ballad entitled 'Bonnie Bessie Lee'" (digital.nls.uk/broadsides/broadside/cfm/id/14872/transcript).

471. In the Doric dialect of northeastern Scotland this refers to a young man or lad.

472. This is an excerpt from the song entitled "Bonnie Bessie Lee."

473. Robert Nicholl (1814-1837) was a Scottish poet.

years after they felt certain they had solved a certain problem to their satisfaction that it was simply an impossibility that it could be any other way than they had proved it.

Ezekiel Walters was a young Quaker, a native of the Old Quaker settlement of [S]outh Yarmouth.[474]. He was a young man of frugal habits. Had the good traits of character peculiar to the Society of Friends and it might be he had inherited a few prejudices peculiar to his ancestors.

He was the owner of fifty acres of fairly good land, in the Township above[475] named, and near to the Village of Sparta. Ezekiel wrought hard **[153]** and brought his little farm into an excellent state of cultivation fruit growing being a special factor in his crops. He had eschewed marriage until rather late in the marriageable[476] years, believing that the expense[477] of maintaining a wife and perhaps a family would make severe inroads on his yearly profits. He had seen and thought of many girls of his acquaintance[478], and a kind of theoretical way had in his imagination fancied himself a <u>Benedict</u>.[479] For years he <u>ba[t]ched</u> it. But at last without seeking the opportunity of meeting a girl, as he thought, suitable to his needs, and his preconceived notions of what his wife should be, a girl turned up that, to use a rude expression, filled his bill. A Quakeress buxom and clean of heart, and of everything else pertaining to a maiden. Ezekiel proposed and was duly accepted. The wedding followed in due time, and she was duly installed in his house to be his everything as Help Mate[480] for him in this life.

It is sel[d]om that the most loving couple have not a skeleton of some kind to come between them (at odd times) to alloy the bliss of marital love. But in the case of Deborah and Ezekiel there was no skeleton to mar the conjugal felicity. The economy of life in all its varied concomitants was reduced to scientific principles.

That the ways of society (in the twentieth century) and as expressed in the Township of Y[armouth] was fast declining into that state of voluptuousness[481] that ruined the great nations and cities of antiquity. They were determined to do whatever lay in their power to avert this calamity as long as they lived.

---

474. South Yarmouth is in the state of Massachusetts. There was a Quaker community there during the 19th century.

475. AB "aboved."

476. AB "marriagable."

477. AB "expence."

478. AB "acquantance."

479. He is referring here to St. Benedict (c. 480–c. 547), the founder of Western monasticism.

480. AB "Help Meet."

481. AB "volumptuousness."

In the ordinary course of nature (one year after the wedding) there came a fine baby boy. Providence had been generous. He was a sturdy little fellow and the fond parents were determined [154] to train him up to assist at least in renovating the existing evils of the times. He was to be trained up in the way he should go with faith that when he was old he would not depart from it. John grew up to school age, and gave many proofs of a discriminating mind. He developed a genius for surgery, and a knowledge of medicinal plants, and how to compound an elixir from them and when his mother's chickens got sick could apply the required antidote. When a leg was broken, John would set it and apply the splints with surprising skill and Ezekiel and Deborah were convinced it would be a downright sacrifice of talent, and serious loss to the world at large to bring up John a farmer, and resolved to educate him for the medical profession. Accordingly John was sent to school, in the Village of S[outh Yarmouth]. Although a Quaker settlement there was a number of the younger generation tinged with the degenerating bias towards apostasy of the orthodox Quakerism in polity and costume. Especially was this the case with the young girls, who in some way merged into a kind of evolution into the fashions of the times unknown to mothers and daughters of the previous generation.

Every boy remembers his first day at school as long as he lives. It often has a bearing on his future career. His home spun, home made costume from the top or crown of his head to his stoga[482] boots was a source of[483] merriment to the boys and girls of the school. He suffered much mental anguish from the scoffs and jibes[484] of the scholars especially the girls who teased, and ta[u]nted him about breaking his mother's apron strings. John had no secrecy from his mother, and told her every evening his grievances, how the girls had made fun of his clothes and being tied to her apron strings. His mother advised him never to mind them nor what they said, they were only butterflies, no good whatever [155] would never be any good, to their parents, themselves or anyone else but a bill of expense to the unfortunate man who married them, and a hindrance[485] to every good cause. A very old saying though somewhat threadbare from repetition, is it is hard to take out of the flesh what is bred in the bone. So it was with John Walters, he grew up with a very low opinion of the female genus homa. He however licked the bully of the school and championed the rights of the smaller scholars and notwithstanding his rather uncourtly dress and manner, it soon became known he had a bone in his sleeve and brains in his head. Fain would the ambitious maiden sidle up to him to get a pointer

---

482. This is a short form for Conestoga, associated with the Pennsylvania home of the Quakers. It refers to the work boots that they wore.

483. AB "merriement."

484. AB "gibes."

485. AB "hinderance."

on some question she could not solve herself.

He fought his way up to be the best scholar in the school, and passed the Entrance almost without an error, and received the plaudits of Teacher, Trustees and the Section generally. He passed on rapidly from high school to University, then Medical College, and came out a full fledged M.D. with M.A. and several other letters indicating his great skill in healing.

He hung out his first <u>shingle</u> in a small Town in North Middlesex[486] and soon became popular as a successful Doctor. Much sought after as a Physician, but as a man hated by the women. When he made a call to see a sick patient, even if there was no contagion, he would invariably examine their <u>sink</u>, smell about it, look downstairs if there was a cellar, and order certain sanitary[487] measures to be applied as soon as possible.

After a few years practise in L,[488] he became an authority in many diseases, especially diphtheria,[489] scarlet fever, typhoid fever and the many diseases of children. Inducements were offered him to move to London where his sphere of action would be much larger and the medical college and hospitals would be great benefited by **[156]** his advanced opinions, also important to the medical fraternity of the city.

In accordance with these inducements Doctor Walters removed to London. Purchased a lot in a new street in south London and built a cottage according to his own idea of architecture, for health and convenience. On the a[d]joining lot a Lawyer had a short time previous established himself in a neat cottage. Both bachelors, and opposed to wedlock, and women on general principles, Mr Manton the lawyer had a housekeeper, known as (old Sarah) who attended to his household affairs. He was almost a slave to his profession, dabbled in politics, just as far as it came in contact with courts of Law. As for the church, it brought him nothing, and he gave it nothing, unless it came within the ear of the law. Dr. Walters [was] just [as] the lawyer, but the affairs of church and state received a fair share of his leisure time. The Dr. had a housekeeper also who attended to his domestic affairs, in the person of a middle aged widow Mrs Brown who served him as an automaton for he never spoke to her unless dire necessity required it.

The Dr. and law[y]er became fast friends. Although almost antithetical in appearance and mentally yet they were staunch friends, and associated as brothers. The lawyer told the Dr. of his intricacies[490] in law affairs, the quibbles, quirks and subtle means to gain a case. The Dr told the man of

486. This is in Middlesex County, in southwestern Ontario, that is centred around the city of London.

487. AB "sanatary."

488. I suspect that this is used to indicate the 19th century hamlet of Lieury, which Uncle Alex would be hesitant to try to spell.

489. AB "dipheria."

490. AB "intricasies."

law, in confidence of course, the many foibles and superstitious notions he had to contend with in his practise. They often passed the evenings in pleasant discussions on the leading topics of the day. The Dr. was a frequent contributor[491] to the Medical Journal and Lancet and, germs, and microbes were the bane of the human race.

As the Dr. sat in his front room one summer afternoon meditating [157] on a dangerous case of typhoid, and several far gone with tuberculosis, a carriage drove up to the front of Manton's cottage. The driver leaped from his seat, opened the carriage door and out spring a fairy form, a vision of frills, lace, and fabulous, by name unknown to the human male. A hat high above her head, like a collection of gossamer[492] streamers waved by an evening zephyr, made almost a halo around a shapely head. She stood on the curb beautiful in her summer drapery, while the coachman handed out trunks, valises, telescopes, handboxes, grips[493] and bags of many shapes and sizes. The Doctor had heard in some indefinite way that Manton had a sister. Could this possibly be her? He had associated her in his imagination as a skranky old maid (like Sarah Brass[494] as described by Dickens whose scapulas were sticking out in bold relief from her back). But here was a lady of the latest fashion from the crown of her head to her dainty slippered feet. He wondered what place in the great economy of life this creature was to fill. Surely the Mighty Maker of all things had made an inadvertent mistake in the creation of many woman, but this one was beyond the wildest imagination.

As he gazed in a pitiful reverie[495] at this seeming airy form, Old Sarah came flying down the walk to the street all in dishabille her hair floating behind her like a branch in a tempest. She seized the lady in her arms lifted her to the level of her own face and seemed to devour her more like bites, than kisses. "God help the genus homo in the future" exclaimed the Doctor audibly. The terrier dog came running across the lawn to the street, he had no tail to wag, but he wagged his hindquarters with vigour. The young lady lifted Sancho up and kissed him as an ardent lover kisses his dearly beloved after a long absence.

The exhibition of exuberant[496] affection for Sancho disgusted this Dungeon of learning,[497] and he groaned inwardly at such nonsense.

491. AB "contributer."

492. AB "gossemer."

493. AB "gripes."

494. Sally (Sarah) Brass is a minor character in Charles Dickens' *Old Curiosity Shop* (1841), the sister of a lawyer.

495. AB "revery."

496. AB "exuberent."

497. This expression comes from the Scots writer Sir John Carr (1772–1832), a lawyer and travel writer.

The lawyer informed his young Sister that the Doctor was a profound thinker, a great authority on the science of medicine. His mind soared above the society of women generally, but especially young ladies, and eschewed their company as much as possible, that she should not flirt, no remain in his company when he comes over here to converse with me. Helen Manton had just graduated from a young lady's Seminary, and full of young life in all its varied emotional acumen tossed her shapely little head and said "he will seek my company, before I seek his, Brother."

Time passed on and the Dr. often observed Miss Manton out in the garden among her flowers, humming a tune and giving a snatch of the song as she lightly ran up the steps at the back door. He acknowledged to himself she was the most perfect physical figure of a woman he had ever seen, and he wondered if she took no notice of him. One evening the Lawyer was later than usual in getting home. The Dr. had gone over to have a chat with him on a very important case of cancer that the medical faculty of London was very much interested in. He had taken his seat in t he hall or lobby, had only been seated a few minutes when the rustling of a woman's dress coming down stairs attracted his attention, and before he could think or move, Miss Manton was on his knee and her arm round his neck, showering kisses on his lips and cheeks, interjecting with "you naughty old brother, why have you been so late of coming and I had such a nice supper ready for you. I hope it is not spoiled yet." With this she jumped from his knee and away. The man of science was stun[n]ed, stultified as if a lightning[498] bolt has struck the house. He rose and stole away to his own house. "She thought I was her brother. What will I do, what will she think of her conduct if she learns the truth.["] He went to bed, he forgot the case of the cancer, reflecting on the nice **[159]** soft arm round his neck, it felt so awful[499] pleasant, and the kisses were an experience fraught with unalloyed bliss, that he longed for a repetition of the same. No female lips had sipped the nectar from his own. His mother had kissed him over and over again, but the feeling was not the same. When he entered the sick rooms as he went his rounds he observed flowers and dainties by the patients as if by some canny hand. He asked "Who did this, who gave you this, Miss Manton, Miss Manton?" The creature has some good about her after all. As he walked along the street Miss Manton was walking alongside of him. As he looked in some standard author for some dangerous case, Miss Manton looked straight in his face. "Confound it, what is the matter with me?" The Doctor was a true son of old Adam notwithstanding his scientific, and philosophic knowledge. A young man in Manton's office came over occasionally in an evening to accompany Helen on the [piano] with [tenor]. This seemed to grieve the Doctor. "What could that young Jackanapes of

498. AB "lightening."

499. AB "aweful."

a young lawyer want[500] coming here? Manton took the man of healing on these occasions to the upstairs parlour to be away from the music, but the Dr. seemed absent and uneasy. His heretofore opinions of girls, in fact all the female genus homa was fading away, he was very loath to believe his mother wrong.

One day Helen was busy in her garden, humming low and sweetly. "Where ye gang awa Jamie?"[501] The Doctor could stand it no longer, he [went] out and into his own garden, strode across the division hedge, and said, "Can't I help you with that.["] "Why yes you can,["] in tones so pleasant that Doctor John Walters was not only fas[c]inated, but his doom was sealed. He married this flibbertigibbet[502] in less than a year, and Ezekiel and Deborah came up to south London to welcome their grandson in fashionable attire

THE END

BACK STORIES OF CHAPTER NINETEEN

It is difficult to figure out where this story comes from. It does not relate to the farm, Whitchurch or Markham townships or even to Toronto. Uncle Alex moved to the Dorchester area, in East Middlesex, in 1865, so it must have taken place sometime after that. Doctor John Walters might have been a friend of his from those days, and shared this story with him, with Uncle Alex putting his own interpretation on it. There was a famous Dr. John Walters in the second half of the 19th century and the early 20th century who was British. He was an army doctor for a short while in Hamilton, where he met his first wife (named Mary).

---

500. AB "wanted."

501. This is the first line of a song written or collected by Lady Carolina Oliphant Nairne (1766–1845), a Scottish poet, song writer and collector.

502. AB "flipperty gibbet." The word has a long history in the English language meaning someone, usually a young woman, who is flighty, whimsical or a gossip. It is onomatopoeic.

References Cited

"A Brief History of the Town of Newmarket," www.newmarket.ca/Thingstodo/Document/History%20-%20Terry%20Carter%20Compilation.pdf.

Annual Report of the Minister of Agriculture and Food, Ontario, 45th Annual Report, Sessional Papers, vol. 23, part 2, pp. 27–30, 1890.

Anonymous, 1878, *Notes and Queries: A Medium of Intercommunication for Literary Men, General Readers, Etc.*, fifth series, vol. 10, July–December, London: John Francis. (Referenced contributors: p. 47, Alexander Paterson; p. 196, John Pickford; p. 235, "GSD."

Armstrong, Frederick H., 1988, *A City in the Making: Progress, People and Perils in Victorian Toronto*, Toronto: Dundurn Press.

Berleth, Richard, 2010, *Bloody Mohawk: The French and Indian War and American Revolution on New York's Frontier*, New York: Black Dome Press.

Bilson, Geoffrey, 1977, "The First Epidemic of Asiatic Cholera in Lower Canada 1832," *Medical History*, pp. 411–33.

Blodget, Lorin, 1857, *Climatology of the United States of the temperate latitudes of North American continent, embracing a full comparison of these with the climatology of the temperate latitudes of Europe and Asia et al.*, Philadelphia: J. B. Lippincott & Co. (babel.hathitrust.org/cgi/pt?id=njp.32 101073304436;view=1up;seq=5).

Brock, James Daniel, "Henderson, Alexander (1824–87)," in *Dictionary of Canadian Biography*, vol. 11, University of Toronto/Université Laval, 2003–, accessed April 10, 2018 (http://www.biographi.ca/en/bio/henderson_alexander_1824_87_11E.html).

Buchan, Peter, 1819, *Annals of Peterhead, from its foundation to the present time* (reprinted through Bibliolife Network).

Campey, Lucille H., 2002, *"Fast Sailing and Copper-Bottomed": Aberdeen Sailing Ships and the Emigrant Scots They Carried to Canada 1774–1855*, Toronto: Natural Heritage Books.

Campey, Lucille H., 2002, *The Scottish Pioneers of Upper Canada: Glengarry and Beyond*, Toronto: Natural Heritage Books.

Carter, Robert T., 2014, *Stories of the Rebellion of 1837 in Old York County: Newmarket—Heart of the 1837 Yonge Street Rebellion*, Newmarket: Newmarket Historical Society Occasional Paper Series.

Cattermole, William, 1831, *Emigration, the advantages of emigration to Canada, the substance of two lectures.* (https://archive.org/stream/emigrationadvan00cattgoog/emigrationadvan00cattgoog-djvu.txt)

Cruikshank, George and Robert Cruikshank, 1825, *The Universal Songster, or Museum of Mirth: forming the most complete, extensive, and* valuable collection of ancient and modern songs in the English language, London.

Da Silva, Maria and Andrew Hind, 2010, *Rebels against Tories in Upper Canada 1837*, Toronto: James Lorimer & Company Ltd.

Dent, John Charles, 1885, *The Story of the Upper Canada Rebellion*, vol. 2, Toronto: C. Blackett Robinson.

Dobson, David and Kit Dobson, 2009, *Ships from Scotland to North America, 1830-1860*, vols. 1 and. 2, Baltimore: Clearfield Company.

Ferguson, William, 1881, *The Great North of Scotland Railway: A Guide*, Edinburgh: David Douglas.

Jameson, Anna Brownell, 1965 [1838], *Winter Studies and Summer Rambles in Canada*, Toronto: McClelland & Stewart.

Mackey, Frank, 2000, *Steamboat Connections Montreal to Upper Canada*, Montreal and Kingston: McGill-Queen's University Press.

Moodie, Susanna, 2000 [1913], *Roughing it in the Bush or Forest Life in Canada*, Toronto: Prospero.

Mulvany, Charles Pelham, Graeme Mercer Adam and Christopher Blackett Robinson, 1885, *History of Toronto and County of York, Ontario*, vol. 1, Toronto: C. Blackett Robinson.

my.tbay.tel/bmartin/Jenkins.htm. Most of this was taken from the *Papers and Records* of the Ontario Historical Society, vol. 27, 1931, pp. 15–76.

my.tbay.tel/bmartin/milia.htm. From information originally published by the Ontario Historical Society, Papers and Records, vol. 1, 1899, pp. 132–8 regarding Captain Cameron's Company of the Regiment of York.

Otto, Stephen, 2006, "Where the Bodies are Buried," *The Fife and Drum: The Newsletter of the Friends of Fort York and Garrison Common*, vol. 10, no. 4, December, p. 1.

Paterson, Alexander, 1901, *Memories of Monquhitter: or Reminiscences of the Early Forties*, Banff: Banffshire Journal Office, in Banff.

Reaman, George Elmore, 1971, *A History of Vaughan Township*, Vaughan Township Historical Society, printed by Toronto: University of Toronto Press (www.ourroots.ca/e/toc.aspx?id=8222). See picture of left-handed plow, image 0057 between pages 36 and 37.

Robertson, John Ross, 1974 [1898], *Landmarks of Toronto*, vol. 3, Belleville: Mika Publishing.

Roland, Charles G., "Robert Charles Horne," *Dictionary of Canadian Biography*, vol. 7 (1836–1850), (www.biographi.ca/en/bio/horne_robert_charles_7E.html).

Ruggle, Richard E., 2003, "Mortimer, George," in *Dictionary of Canadian Biography*, vol. 78, Toronto/Quebec: University of Toronto/Université Laval, accessed March 18, 2016 (www.biographi.ca/en/bio/mortimer_george_7E.html).

Steckley, John, 2014, *The Eighteenth Century Wyandot: A Clan Based Study*, Waterloo: Wilfrid Laurier University Press.

Sutherland, Gavin, "The Peterhead Whalers, 1788-1893," www.nefa.net/archive/peopleandlife/sea/pheadwhalers.htm).

Sutherland, Gavin, 1993, *The Whaling Years: Peterhead (1788–1893)*, Aberdeen: Centre for Scottish Studies, University of Aberdeen.

The Word on the Street, Broadside Ballad entitled 'Bonnie Bessie Lee'" (digital.nls.uk/broadsides/broadside/cfm/id/14872/transcript).

Toronto Directory, 1837, www.statictorontopubliclibrary.ca/da/pdfs/706129.pdf.

Traill, Catharine Parr, 2004 [1836], *The Backwoods of Canada: Being Letters from the Wife of an Emigrant Officer, Illustrative of the Domestic Economy of British America*, Project Gutenberg (originally London: Charles Knight).

Turing, John, 2016, "Conservatives and Conditional Loyalty: The Rebellion Losses Crisis of 1849 in Montreal," *British Journal of Canadian Studies*, vol. 29, no. 1, March, pp. 83–103.

University of Minnesota Libraries, *Collection of ballads, songsheets*, 1805–1840[?], vol. 1, *The Bold Irishman* (http://sites.google.com/a/umn.edu/mh/home/Irishman-html.)

Worrall, John, 1877, *Worrall's Directory of the North-Eastern Counties of Scotland: Comprising the Counties of Forfar, Fife, Kinross, Aberdeen, Banff and Kincardine*, Oldham: J. Worrall.

www.barbaradickson.ca/david-cragg/st-lawrence-rapids.
www.biographi.ca/en/bio/mortimer_george_7E.html.
www.froglife.org/amphibians-and-reptiles/common-frog-2/.
www.lostrivers.ca/content/points/Notes.html.
www.onekind.org/education/animals_a_ostrich.
www.rampantscotland.com/songs/blsongs_tamson.htm.

www.ingramcontent.com/pod-product-compliance
Lightning Source LLC
Chambersburg PA
CBHW030908080526
44589CB00010B/203